Manipulation in the Disclosure of the *Securitate* Files

STUDIES IN POLITICS, SECURITY AND SOCIETY

Edited by Stanisław Sulowski
Faculty of Political Science and International Studies
University of Warsaw

VOLUME 39

Alina Petra Marinescu

Manipulation in the Disclosure of the *Securitate* Files

The Case of Mona Muscă

Bibliographic Information published by the Deutsche Nationalbibliothek
The Deutsche Nationalbibliothek lists this publication in
the Deutsche Nationalbibliografie; detailed bibliographic
data is available in the internet at http://dnb.d-nb.de.

Library of Congress Cataloging-in-Publication Data
A CIP catalog record for this book has been applied for
at the Library of Congress.

Cover illustration: Courtesy of Benjamin Ben Chaim.

This publication was financially supported by the Faculty of Communication
and International Relations, "Danubius" University of Galați.

ISSN 2199-028X
ISBN 978-3-631-85700-7 (Print)
E-ISBN 978-3-631-85729-8 (E-PDF)
E-ISBN 978-3-631-85756-4 (EPUB)
DOI 10.3726/b18542

© Peter Lang GmbH
Internationaler Verlag der Wissenschaften
Berlin 2021
All rights reserved.

Peter Lang – Berlin · Bern · Bruxelles · New York ·
Oxford · Warszawa · Wien

All parts of this publication are protected by copyright. Any
utilisation outside the strict limits of the copyright law, without
the permission of the publisher, is forbidden and liable to
prosecution. This applies in particular to reproductions,
translations, microfilming, and storage and processing in
electronic retrieval systems.

This publication has been peer reviewed.

www.peterlang.com

Contents

Argument 7

CHAPTER I: Information 9
    I.1. Definitions and Theories 9
    I.2. Press Information 13
    I.3. Processing Press Information:
        The Journalistic Text 17

CHAPTER II: Disinformation 21
    II.1. Overview 21
    II.2. Media Disinformation 25

CHAPTER III: Manipulation 41
    III.1. Overview 41
    III.2. Short Classification of Manipulations 47
    III.3. Manipulation through the Media 54

CHAPTER IV: Politics and the Press 69
    IV.1. Relationship Between Politicians
        and the Media 69
    IV.2. Media Crisis and the Social Image 73

CHAPTER V: Case Study 79
    V.1. Media Approach to the Topic of Mona
        Muscă 79
    V.2 Development of Events in the Case of
        Mona Muscă 80

    V.3. Analysis Material 82
    V.4. Methods of Analysis 84
    V.5. Information and Manipulation in the Case of Mona Muscă: Content Analysis 87
    V.6. Analysis of the Headlines That Accompany the Studied Articles 101
    V.7. Analysis of the Images Placed Next to the Researched Articles 103

CHAPTER VI: Conclusions 111

APPENDIX 1 115

APPENDIX 2 119

APPENDIX 3 123

APPENDIX 4 125

Bibliography 127

Index of Names 129

Argument

> These days, power manifests itself less in action than in communication. Whoever communicates better and more efficiently is more influential and, as a consequence, more powerful (Claudiu Săftoiu, 2003, p. 16).

Around 1800, theorist Edmund Burke started looking at the Reporters' Gallery down in the House of Commons and stated: "there sits a Fourth Estate more important far than they all."

At the time, the press that Burke was looking at had started to manifest its influence towards an audience the researchers now call *mass society*, a homogenous group for whom the process of message selection and interpretation was still little known. The purposes of the mass media messages oscillated between information and serving the interests of a few influential groups.

Less than two hundred years later, we are looking at professional journalism that aims at an equally suited audience. The hundreds of different means of communication speak to well-established audiences, that, despite their diversity, would eventually lean toward the same channel of distribution for the information. As time went by, the roles of the mass media changed and adapted to the individuals' necessities.

The purpose of those who enable mass communication is not so different, however, from the one it had at the dawn of the press. The media message is still used today for two main reasons: information and serving different interests. Words such as *disinformation* or *manipulation*, although only recently entered common vocabulary, have become constant when the mass media is discussed.

The whole phenomenon started to grow once the print press and audio-visual press became the main message carriers of any kind. Whoever wants to influence the masses to obtain certain advantages depend mainly on these means of communication. Politicians are the first to appreciate visibility and propaganda as essential to maintain their privileged positions.

The politicians' interest in the mass media is explainable, nevertheless, through the constant preoccupation of the media owners in gaining profit and leading more prosperous businesses. And the one thing that is constant in this process is the audience. The mass audience, whose preferences for a certain media station or for voting for a certain candidate are the objectives desired by both parties.

Disinformation and manipulation are two of the most well-known ways of influencing public opinion according to the interests of a certain group or person. Politicians disinform the press, the press manipulates politicians, and the audience is usually subjected to campaigns meant to transmit the information only in the form that is required by one or both parties when their interests coincide.

Deontologically speaking, the main purpose of journalism is information, not changing the audience's perception for someone's benefit. This argument is what stands behind this book.

At the time when her files were declassified, Mona Muscă was seen as one of the most respected politicians in Romania, which reflected in the polls and research done during her press campaigns. At the end of 2006, the people's trust in Mona Muscă had dropped from 60 to 29 %. The forums of the online publications were only highlighting negative opinions of her, as opposed to the months before August 2006. Between August and November, the events that connected her – at the time a member of the House of Deputies – with the Securitate police started a series of media scandals, and hundreds of op-eds. and news showed up on this subject.

The polling results already mentioned, as well as the research into who might have been interested in ousting her from politics, were the foundations of the analyses, which had the following purpose: determining the extent to which the press objectively presented the facts or, on the contrary, manipulated public opinion in the case of Mona Muscă.

CHAPTER I: Information

I.1. Definitions and Theories

The term *information* has been used in many different domains and can convey different meanings, depending on its purpose. Claude-Jean Bertrand considers that information is "data stocks (messages, signals, symbols) that receive meaning through the process of communication. Communication allows the human being to create new meanings, to interpret the messages and to transform ideas and knowledge through a dialogue of peers" (2001, p. 21).

According to the *Larousse Media Dictionary*, the word *information* has three meanings, each leaving room for interpretations or representations with very different connotations. The first meaning is that of a "statement or set of statements on someone or something likely to be communicated to one or more persons, located in one place or scattered" (2005, p. 170). This first meaning is also the one that was the basis of the information theory, developed in 1947 by Claude E. Shannon and Warren Weaver.

"This theory aims to break down any communication of information into several elements, from its source to its destination, as it passes through the media or channel that ensures its transmission after encoding the signal, for the receiver that decodes it to find the initial signal" (C.J. Bertrand, 2001, p. 171). This model applied to media communication was inspired by that of Harold D. Lasswell and was completed in the 1950s by other researchers, who concluded that this scheme is too simplistic, that it does not contain data on its content and significance, featuring the recipient as a passive source. They concluded that "the feedback process was often decisive, and that communication requires ... a relationship between sender and receiver, which produces a certain type of effect in a given context" (C.J. Bertrand, 2001, p. 20). Subsequent research has added the idea of encoding and decoding, referring to "the new translation of the message that the receiver makes, extracting the necessary meanings" (C.J. Bertrand, 2001, p. 20).

The second meaning is given by adding the definite article to the noun *information* ("the information"), which is considered to designate a completely different reality, that of a "unique institution with techniques, professionals, and disciplines, which appeared in the nineteenth century, along with the industrial revolution and the struggle for political and personal freedoms." This meaning is closely linked to those areas of journalism that place fiction and entertainment in the background and are primarily dedicated to informing the audience. The information is defined, this time, concerning credible statements and knowledge. "Information, as content broadcast through the media – a newspaper, a radio station – is a set of news, statements, announcements or events that have been given a meaning, through a certain form and perspective, to be easily accessible to the public. Knowledge is a more or less exact science, with a more general perspective, whose specific connection with reality is assimilated as such by a group or an individual" (*Larousse Media Dictionary*, p. 2005 171). In this case, the role of information is precisely to create a connection between current events and the audience and to develop and facilitate the process of knowledge. Therefore, journalistic practice delivers the information in the form of news or other types of press materials, in a way that is accessible to receivers.

The third meaning conferred by the Media Dictionary took shape by the end of the twentieth century and describes, according to Fritz Machlup and Marc U. Porat a wide range of elements that constitute the news (recent events), the economic, financial, and social fields (data), but also entertainment in technological form and general knowledge. The meaning of the term information develops under the influence of new media and gives rise to new activities and even new fields of enterprise. In 1992, the Vice President of the United States of America, Al Gore introduced the phrase *information superhighway*, "the only guarantee to removing the challenges of industrial development, education, health, and communication." This later turned into the *information society*. Used by politicians and international officials, this expression "designates both a reality and a project," referring to the place of prime importance that information has gained to the detriment of industry or agriculture but also the imminent evolution of society due to the progress made in the field of communication.

"The phrase *information society* seems to have been trivialized by excessive use, but many definitions have not also brought a long-awaited increase in clarity. What is certain is that *information* and *the process of informing* have become the function and logic of institutions of overwhelming importance, both subjects and objects of major interest." (Nasty Vlădoiu, 2005, p. 66). The same author considers that a piece of information cannot be observed as such if the conventions and constraints that determine it, as well as the facts and events that it relates to, are not fully understood. "In other words: previous knowledge is needed to circumscribe the meaning of the information" (Vlădoiu, 2005, p. 68).

In the absence of a specific context, independent information cannot survive because it makes no sense. Moreover, it is only an abstract notion that the receiver does not even bother to store. Nonetheless, information responds to people's vital needs, like having a roadmap in society and offering the input necessary for decision-making and building relationships with others. In this sense, Mireille Rădoi points out that the following seven aspects of information can be distinguished:

- actors (who?) – organizations, institutional structures, interest groups, people
- content (what?) – reference to the essence, not to the phenomenon, the activity, the product
- spatial (where?) – location of the entity or action, details related to the destination
- temporal (when?) – the date and time of the phenomenon
- action (how?) – the quantitative-qualitative approaches and the means of development
- deterministic-motivational (why?) – the real causality of the event
- projective (with what consequences?) – post-factual, an appreciation of the effects as well as of its possible and probable evolution.

It's noticeable that the aspects associated with information, in general, are the same as in the case of press news, so any discussion regarding press information can be extrapolated to information in a broad sense and vice versa. This is also because the individual is subjected to a continuous process of information, a process in which the press only plays a small part, and whose actors change from hour to hour. "Informing someone means putting them in touch with something, making a certain event known to them. Being informed involves a state (of knowing) and an event (of which you are at a certain point informed about). If the information is summarized, it does not mean that the state has changed, but only the event. The information selects and changes the states of a system, depending on the structure ..., eliminating uncertainty about the world" (N. Vladoiu, 2005, p. 69).

In his study, *A Mathematical Theory of Communications* (1948), Claude Shannon defines information by probability. According to this theory, information becomes relevant only when it has unexpected, surprising content. Once the event in question has a very high degree of predictability, the information becomes nil (N. Vlădoiu, 2005, p. 69).

To conclude, the informative value is what legitimizes the transmitted message and determines the extent to which the receiver chooses to receive it or ignore it. The value of information depends firstly on the characteristics and expectations of the receiver and secondly on each domain and context.

To be able to issue useful messages which are appropriate to each institution or person, Mireille Rădoi analyzes the use of information, in her class notes shared by N. Vlădoiu, and determines that it depends on several factors (2005, p. 71–73).

1. Characteristics of information

Decision-makers tend to value information from personal verbal reports rather than from formal, written documents. They also tend to remember information expressed in a language that reflects specific political issues rather than information asserted in an abstract manner or wooden language. Decision-makers inadvertently pay more attention to the information they perceive as objective, accurate, precise, and apply it to other similar issues.

2. The means of investigation

The means used to produce and interpret the information must comply with quality standards. ... The information must also take into account organizational constraints, the most important of which would be the need for timely information.

3. The structure of the problem

The way the problem is defined and structured influences the extent to which information is used by decision-makers: relatively well-structured issues involve some consensus on objectives, goals, alternatives, and consequences, rather than less structured ones.

4. The political and bureaucratic apparatus

The interference of political elites, the bureaucratization of certain positions, the formalization of the procedures, and the propensity to conservatism shown by some systems that amend or even punish innovation – all contribute to the underuse or neutralization of information that originates from some analyses and evaluations.

5. Interactions between the actors

The nature and type of relationships between the people engaged in any way in the action, process, or operation about which they are informed influences the use of the information. ... The purpose and intensity of the interactions between those involved dictate how information is produced, transformed, and used.

In support of the classification made by Mireille Rădoi comes Roger Clausse, who identifies in the *Explanatory Dictionary of Journalism, Public Relations, and Advertising* some of the traits of quality information. He suggests three categories of attributes: "essential – truth, objectivity and lack of self-interest; professional – universality, speed, conciseness, originality and variety and social – the social significance of the related fact, the precision of its subject, the integrity, the actuality, and the accessibility" (Cristian Florin Popescu, 2002, p. 69).

I.2. Press Information

As pointed out above, by defining the term information, a word specific to the media field was created, since the 19th century, a word that should represent the basis of the journalistic method. Many theorists have considered information to be one of the basic functions performed by the media. Malcolm Wiley and Dennis McQuail have centered even more media functions around the ability to inform. The former, quoted by Coman, considers that the press fulfills five functions: "to provide information, to analyze information, to give a general frame of reference for knowledge, to entertain and to disseminate encyclopedic knowledge" (1999, p. 73). McQuail opts for two types of functions: for society as a whole and each individual (1999, p. 73). Both categories place the information function, which we will discuss further, in the first place.

The other functions of the media will be analyzed in detail in the chapter "Disinformation," in the subchapter "Disinformation Through the Media."

The information function is centered on "the need of individuals and groups to control their environment; based on the information they receive through the media, people assess the importance of events that could directly interest them, anticipate some of the trends of the economic, social or political life and make certain decisions being fully aware of the facts" (Mihai Coman, 1999, p. 73).

To highlight the components of proper journalistic information, Cristian Florin Popescu proposes a discussion about under-information and over-information, citing the definitions given by Andres Freund.

Under-information is "truncated or even non-existent information on important topics" (2002, p. 373). Popescu likens a journalistic text of this type to a file or a press statement.

Concerning over-information, Freund says that it is defined by an increased interest in some events to the detriment of others, of greater importance. "It is a diversion that creates confusion, trivializes dramatic events, and is dizzying with its abundance of insignificant details. Unnecessary detail is specific to over-information" (A. Freund in C.F. Popescu, 2002, p. 374).

Andreas Freund showcased, in the same work *Journalisme et Mesinformation,* the term *para information,* which he defined as "a thinned, approximate, minor version of the information ... Through para information, information is replaced by images with relative and diminished meanings, by sensationalism or by personalizing a problem that does not refer to people" (1991, p. 263).

"By contrast, correct information is most often expressed in a neutral tone. This superficially signals the reader of the journalist's non-involvement, of the fact that the journalist commands the event ... Once these conditions are met, the chances of its credibility increase unhindered" (C.F. Popescu, 2005, p. 140).

In 1947, American sociologist Kurt Lewin suggested the term *gatekeepers,* associated with journalists. But journalists not only have the simple role of guarding the informational gates but also of deciding what information deserves to be turned into news and transmitted to receivers and what does not. The press has control over the message it filters according to certain well-defined criteria, which confer it the *value of information.* Of these, Melvin Mancher considers six as the most important, about the receiver or the target audience: temporal proximity, spatial proximity, unusual facts, conflict, consequences, capturing human interest (1991, pp. 54–64).

According to David Randall, "the role of a newspaper is to discover fresh information on matters of public interest and to pass it on to readers as quickly and as accurately as possible, honestly and in a balanced way. That's all. The newspaper can ... tell readers what it thinks about the latest films, how potatoes are grown or why the government should resign. But without fresh information, we would only have opinions on things we already know. Interesting, maybe even stimulating; but a comment is not news. Information is" (1998, p. 37).

"Of the flow of messages that enter our homes daily, only some provide information of immediate use (weather, prices, cultural events, public transport, etc.). Other bits refer to facts and processes less related to our immediate environment: the news about a coup in a country thousands of kilometers away, about the discovery of a planet ... they do not influence our lives and do not provide us with a foothold for everyday decisions. Instead, all this information forms a specific cultural repertoire, that is added to the symbolic representations and value systems acquired through other channels and from other experiences; this set of knowledge and beliefs contributes to the creation of that conception of the world on which all of the individuals' daily decisions are based" (M. Coman, 1999, p. 74).

Depending on the impact it has on the target audience, information is classified in *Introduction to the Media System* into three broad categories: general, instrumental, and preemptive.

General information refers to the data that the individual does not necessarily need to make their way through society, but only to be able to observe and understand the environment around them. The baggage of knowledge that an individual accumulates daily helps them hold a position about certain situations. "Although we are not specialists, we follow the stock market, the evolution of inflation ... new scientific discoveries, etc. Gathered in the depths of our memory, they provide information capital, which can be updated at any time, to evaluate an event and to establish a strategy." (M. Coman, 1999, p. 74). Over time, the individual becomes unable to filter the informational flow on their own, as it is exhausting, but essential, to adapt to a complex and constantly evolving society.

This is where the institutions responsible for gathering information step in, as they process it to make it accessible and transmit it to the public, fulfilling a mediation role that both facilitates the recipient's access to the message and deprives them of a series of direct experiences, more customary to traditional societies. "A journalistic text published in a Romanian daily is written to be received by a certain segment of Romanian readers, geographically located with a certain precision. ... The journalistic text does not provide raw information, like, for example, the minutes of a meeting. It is first processed by the journalist, in a way that meets the expectations of the public" (Luminița Roșca, 2001, p. 100).

Paul Lazarsfeld and R.K. Merton, theorists in the sociology of mass communication, argue that the individual feels an increasingly stronger need for information due to the abundance of mass media. The media offers daily, through its countless channels, a wide range of information that provides a "certain version of reality, a media image of events, people and socio-historical circumstances" (M. Coman, p. 74).

Moreover, the messages reach the audience in a continuous flow, not allowing any time for the processing of the information through their own set of beliefs. Lazarsfeld and Merton, quoted by Coman, even believe that the individual can feel strongly deprived of media information: "They come to believe that knowing all about the issue of the day also means doing something to control it. They are informed. They are preoccupied. And they have all sorts of ideas about what should be done. ... An increase in media consumption can, unexpectedly, transform the individual's energies, getting them from a state of active participation to a state of passive knowledge." (1999, pp. 74–75). The two sociologists consider that this passivity of the individual as a result of their oversaturation with information is a *narcotic dysfunction*.

Instrumental information forms the necessary baggage for the individual to permanently control their environment, to position, and to plan their daily routine. Both the written and online press, as well as the audiovisual media, offer the public specialized sections that contain information of immediate use. This includes news about the weather, traffic news, stock market news, etc. The local press provides the largest amount of instrumental information, about homes, gardens, pets, etc., because it satisfies both the need to inform the readers and the need to relax, as the message can be decoded effortlessly.

An experiment conducted in 1945 by sociologist Bernard Berelson pointed out the individual's need for utilitarian information. Thus, following a several-month strike by the print journalists of New York, Berelson published a study called *What Missing the Newspapers Means,* which showed that readers care less about the lack of general information than about the lack of instrumental information (cinema and theater programs, data on public transport or news from stores). The need for immediate useful information was thus highlighted.

Preemptive information. "The press messages show not only what has already happened (retrospective positioning), but also what could happen (prospective vision). Moreover, because the description of an event does not exhaust its implications and consequences, the information provided by the media also includes an anticipatory dimension" (M. Coman, 1999, p. 75).

The preemptive function exercised by the media can be identified, for example, in weather bulletins, when the public is made aware of probable heavy snowfalls or ice. Through the media, the public is informed and prepared to deal with unexpected events such as natural disasters, accidents, or different types of crises. C.R. Wright, quoted by Coman, points out that the media's preemptive function has unexpected social consequences: because the information is accessible to the masses, too, not only to the elites, the warnings transmitted by the press point to an additional function, inspiring an egalitarian perspective within society: everyone has an equal chance to escape the danger thus announced" (M. Coman, 1999, p. 75).

Unfortunately, the masses do not always react to the preventive information received. Some of the behavioral anomalies that often occur, according to M. Coman's classification, are the depreciation of the data transmitted by the media, one obvious example being the smoker who does not trust the warnings of specialists, as well as the paroxysmal amplification of information, "sociologists know that groups and communities distort information, process it, through emotional *slippage,* through rumors, false information or even fabulous *legends.*" The same author considers both panic and indifference to be dysfunctions of the information function.

I.3. Processing Press Information: The Journalistic Text

> *The journalistic text is written by a journalist, hired on a permanent or freelance contract, by a publication that is responsible for following a certain content strategy and for respecting the deontological rules deriving from this contract. The final version of the journalistic text is the result of collecting, selecting, hierarchizing and condensing the information (L. Roşca, 2001, p. 99).*

Linguist Roman Jakobson identified six functions of language: expressive, conative, phatic, referential, poetic, and metalinguistic, and Luminița Roșca postulates that two of these are illustrative of the journalistic text: the phatic function and the referential function. The first capitalizes on the ability of the communication channel to maintain the connection between the sender and the recipient. In communication that is mediated by the mass media, the phatic function is exercised through the characteristics of each medium: graphics, text, page layout, tone, image, and its processing. "The referential function focuses the communication on the referent (the objective reality identified through language). It is relevant in communication designating the constituents of the event (proper names, circumstances of place, time, facts). The referential function is an element that defines any journalistic text" (L. Roșca, 2001, p. 104).

"The text created to inform an audience must be based on information that has been previously fact-checked. All the protagonists of the event must be equally represented. Unverified information must be presented as questionable information (completely unverifiable or unverifiable only for the time being). A rumor must be presented as a rumor. Moreover, what is essential to the information must be delivered in a complete form. Referring to details as essential elements produces a serious distortion" (C.F. Popescu, 2005, p. 138).

To meet all the conditions listed above, the production of the journalistic text must meet several specific conditions. Among them, Luminița Roșca emphasizes the selection of information according to the type of data, the transmission channel, and the type of journalistic text that will result from this effort. When referring to the print press, Albert Kientz points out the originality of the message, its intelligibility, the degree of public involvement (proximity), and the psychological depth of the information. These are features that Roșca identifies in all types of press texts, in *Journalism Manual I* (2001, pp. 100–101). Regarding the psychological depth of the message, Abraham Moles considers that if the information reaches deeper layers (the subconscious) of the human psyche, the probability that it will be remembered is higher.

"There are also other criteria. Some are a matter of tradition: politics and entertainment have long been privileged topics – while topics such as the environment, energy, health, or science have been neglected. Other criteria depend on the nature of the media: the newspaper is local, regional or national, serious or popular" (C.J. Bertrand, 2001, p. 46).

"The journalistic text ... is both a product intended for purchase and use, a medium for essential or desired information and it fulfills a public service function. ... As a result, the information is structured according to the reference system (reading habits, knowledge, interests, future projections) of its audience, as well as the thematic sphere of the event" (L. Roşca, 2001, p. 103). To cover all of these categories, the journalistic text not only provides the audience with information but also with ideas, opinions, entertainment, or educational messages. All of these are presented in different packages in terms of genre and form.

This means that the journalist and the text they create or transmit must be subject to many rules, which arise from various constraints, both internal and external, as well as editorial, commercial, deontological, etc. Each publication has its own editorial policy that the journalist must respect, and they have to write their materials according to a certain template (news, report, etc.). Each type of writing has its own canons meant to help the audience distinguish between types of content and differentiate between opinion and fact.

The journalistic text must meet the needs of the target audience, which is increasingly versatile as a result of the continuous increase of the number of mass media, while, at the same time, not encumbering the customer loyalty of the receivers. McQuail believes that "a media product is a commodity or service sold to potential consumers, in competition with other journalistic products" (D. McQuail in M. Coman, 1999, p. 26).

"Receivers of the media messages do not live in the same area, do not know each other, and often do not share common values, beliefs or political beliefs. The only thing that binds them is their relationship to identical media products" (M. Coman, 1999, p. 24). Bertrand divides the public into three broad categories: a small number of people with a superior cultural level, usually with more financial privilege; the middle classes, which come in higher numbers and substantial income and the under-educated. The media focus their resources on serving the middle class, as they are less present in countries where this category is less represented.

Also, most media channels need to support themselves, which is usually managed by selling space normally allocated for journalistic materials, for advertisement, and facing the inherent pressures exerted by advertisers.

CHAPTER II: Disinformation

II.1. Overview

The term "disinformation" first appeared in Russian after World War II (*dezinformaţia*), and it referred to the capitalist practices aimed at subjugating the proletarian masses. In 1949, the *Russian Language Dictionary* defined the term as *the act of misleading through false information*. "It is significant in this case that while the Soviets attributed these practices to opponents who had not yet discovered them, the word itself already served the cause" (Vladimir Volkoff, 2002, p. 16). In 1972, the word also entered the *Chambers Twentieth Century Dictionary*, published in London, and is defined as *the leaking of deliberately misleading information*. After only two years, amid debates over the nuclear issue, in France, disinformation signified the ignorance in which the public was kept regarding a serious problem.

In the *Explanatory Dictionary of Journalism, Public Relations and Advertising*, C.F. Popescu quotes Henri-Pierre Cathala, who considers that disinformation "involves the concealment of real sources and purposes, as well as the intention to harm, through a distorted representation or a biased interpretation of reality. It is a form of aggression that attempts to go unnoticed. It is a subversive psychological action" (2002, p. 112).

According to Vladimir Volkoff, information involves three variables in which one cannot have absolute confidence: the *informant,* who distorts the initial message according to their perceptions, values, beliefs, a person who, without prior intention, can confuse the splashes from a sprinkler with rain; the *means of communication* whose features can modify or alter the message, like a broken telephone and a recipient with a hearing problem; the *informed* person who, even if provided with the exact information, will have the impulse to distort it by their perceptions, just like the sender.

In the communication process, information cannot keep all of its attributes intact. That is because independent information is an abstract element, which needs an informant to turn into a fact. And Volkoff believes that a fact can be presented in seven different ways: it can be affirmed, denied, silenced, amplified, diminished, approved, or disapproved (1999,

p. 128). Under the influence of any of the listed processes, the information undergoes a kind of change that either strengthens it or discredits it, but it certainly does not preserve it in its entirety.

Short History of Disinformation suggests several methods through which the above processes can be used:

- *Denial of facts* – a practice preferred by the less experienced in disinformation and used when it's impossible for the public to fact-check what happened.
- *Reversal of facts* – or a more commonly used method, *the mixture of truth and falsehood* – in this case, whoever wants to disinform public opinion will mix real facts with false ones, a result that can also be achieved by presenting facts inaccurately.
- *Altering of motives* or *altering of circumstances* – the former can radically change the opinion of the public, who chooses to start from other assumptions when analyzing the facts, while the latter aims to provide mitigating circumstances that can legitimize or even exonerate the person concerned.
- *Blurring,* an alternative to *camouflage* – "this method consists in burying a fact under a pile of other unrelated – and, if possible, more likely to arouse the interest of the public – facts" (V. Volkoff, 1999, p. 131). Camouflage works by spotlighting certain elements and placing others in the shadows to legitimize certain actions.
- *Interpretation* – presenting real facts favorably or unfavorably, depending on the interests of various parties. This particular method is widely used by the press. It is usually associated with *the equal and unequal parts* that we will discuss in more detail in the subchapter *Disinformation through the Media*.
- *Generalization* or *illustration* – the former involves adhesion to a group or segment with which the disinformer identifies, while the latter supports it with arguments.

In his treatise on this "technique that also represents a philosophy," Vladimir Volkoff suggests two definitions for the term *disinformation*. He considers both correct, but prefers the second, believing that it "covers its essential aspects better:"

1. A technique allowing the provision of erroneous general information to third parties, prompting them to commit collective acts or to disseminate the judgments desired by the disinformers (1999, p. 17).
2. Disinformation is a manipulation of public opinion for political purposes, through the use of distorted information (1999, p. 25).

The same author also lists the elements of disinformation:

- conscious manipulation of public opinion, otherwise we would be talking about intoxication
- misappropriated means, otherwise, it would be propaganda;
- political purposes, internal or external, otherwise it would be advertising

The author created this list after introducing us to intoxication, propaganda, and advertising, all processes closely related to disinformation, all designed to ultimately pervert a particular opinion.

The first of the three is defined by the Robert Dictionary, and quoted by Volkoff, as an "insidious action upon the spirit, that aims to legitimize certain opinions, to demoralize, to confuse" (1999, p. 22). Guy Durandin believes that "intoxication is meant to suggest a false synopsis, or even an entire false ideology," an opinion shared by C.F. Popescu (2002, p. 182). "For me [V. Volkoff], the difference between intoxication and disinformation is that the first concerns a general staff, a small group of decision-makers, possibly a commander in chief, whereas disinformation is addressed to the public opinion. It would be self-understood that intoxication is not reserved to the military field: a political party, a bank, a manufacturer, a newspaper can profit by the intoxication, however, the purpose shall always be to determine the people, and not collectives, to act in their disservice." (1999, p. 25).

The Larousse Media Dictionary defines propaganda as a "deliberate action taken to generate certain thoughts, to make an individual or a group of individuals believe or act in a certain way or with a certain intention" (2005, p. 255)"

The definition is reflected in the teachings of Macchiavelli's *Prince*: *the ends justify the means* and *to govern is to influence beliefs*. Septimiu Chelcea writes about *Persuasion versus Propaganda* and quotes Jacques Ellul: "Propaganda is the systematic and conscious attempt to influence perceptions, manipulate cognitions and shape behaviors towards a response that supports the goal desired by the propagandist" (2006, p. 131). "In itself, however, propaganda is neither good nor bad. It can bear a negative connotation depending on the methods used, the goals pursued by the persuasive agent, as well as the social context in which it takes place" (S. Chelcea, 2006, p. 131).

Regarding advertising: "from a psychosociological perspective, it is a form of persuasive communication. It is located at the intersection of economics, psychology, sociology, communication sciences, and marketing. Advertising must inform and persuade" (C. Baylon, X. Mignot in S. Chelcea, 2006, p. 134). "The deliberate emphasis on irrationality brings advertising closer to propaganda, but it is not as *Calvinist*: advertising only praises a product; it hardly ever uses negative references to competing products, because it has only one purpose: to sell, and in this field, unlike politics, drawing even hostile attention to rivals could cause a commercial catastrophe" (V. Volkoff, 1999, p. 22). Chelcea lists the attributes that separate advertising from other forms of communication:

a) it is a commercial transaction;
b) it provides information about ideas, goods, or services;
c) advertising is focused on a target audience, not on a specific person;
d) its goal is to promote (sell, disseminate) ideas, goods, services;
e) the sponsor is publicly known.

Going back to disinformation, Vladimir Volkoff sets down three postulates, applicable in everyday life and valid in any field:

- "information never contains 100 % truth; errors creep in along the way, even if no member of the information chain, from an informant to an informed person, has bad intentions;
- whatever one might think, not only is there no objectivity in information, but any claim to objectivity must be treated with suspicion. It is better personally to listen to both sides first than to send an on-site, so-called impartial observer who will sympathize with one side from the very beginning or will be better paid by other;
- it's reasonable that different witnesses will have different perspectives on the event they witnessed. If their perspectives are too similar, there's something not quite right there." (1999, p. 15)

"Objectivity can only exist, even more so in scientific information, where the same experiment, conducted by different scientists, will always lead to the same results." (V. Volkoff, 1999, p. 15)

II.2. Media Disinformation

Vladimir Volkoff advances the hypothesis that "the media is prone to disinformation by its very function, which is to sell information that can seduce, interest, shock, tickle, scare pleasantly before gently calming, in a nutshell, the most pleasant information available. It is easy for the disinformer to make fiction more attractive than the truth, even by – an important point – making it easier to understand and assimilate" (1999, p. 163). The author finds common ground in both information and disinformation. in the shape of emotion, which is easier for the journalist to sell than information, and which the disinformer needs to determine the actions he wants.

Vladimir Volkoff spotlights a paradox that arose along with Gutenberg's invention and spread "in the contemporary and democratic vicious circle: the more public opinion matters, the more information it demands; the more information it receives, the more it matters. However, information is corrupted by the dose of disinformation mixed along with it" (1999, p. 39).

The same author believes that, in its initial form, disinformation was closely linked to propaganda and he provides the following case for illustration: "In 1964, department D [a KGB sector dealing with disinformation activities, which became A in 1968] printed a series of anti-American pamphlets with titles like *America Colonized Twenty Million Blacks* or the *Americans, Our Best Friends,* in which the United States was pictured as the most racist country in the world and an enemy of darker-skinned ethnicities. Initially, these brochures were intended for the Third World. But there is also a second, more subtle intention to all this, which proves that we are in the realm of disinformation. ... The right-wing candidate for the presidency of the Republic is often nominated in these pamphlets, so the American left used them to its advantage, thus becoming the ideal sounding board for the KGB ... some of these brochures were sent in envelopes by the United Information Agency" (1999, p. 164).

Another important example provided by Volkoff is that of the *letters from readers,* a common section in both large and small dailies, that are often published even if they contradict the newspaper's editorial policy and become the origin of certain messages that become very popular for the public opinion. The same mechanism can be used by the audiovisual press as well, that of "a theme that arose in an obscure show, in connection with an innocuous pretext, and will be rebroadcast, ... during a show with a large audience" (1999, p. 165).

Ironically, there are cases in which the media inadvertently disinforms due to the context in which the message is received, as was the case of a radio show whose broadcast has been the subject of countless debates. An unintentional act that later became the basis for the first sociological research on panic behavior induced by the mass media. "With Marconi's invention [the radio] added to Gutenberg's, which in turn had been added to word-of-mouth, disinformation bloomed" (V. Volkoff, 1999, p. 70). In 1938, when more than 80 % of homes in the US owned a radio, Orson Wells broadcast a radio version of the novel *War of the Worlds.* "In this case, the public's anxiety had been exacerbated by the numerous live radio broadcasts from various European capitals haunted by the horrors of war ..., all climaxing with the signing of the Munich Agreement when the American public could hear a variation of dizzying and conciliatory voices ... Against this background of unrest, H.G. Wells' text, performed by Orson Wells, was no longer perceived as fiction, but as proof that the war had even reached America" (M. Coman, 1999, p. 111).

Based on this event, the sociologist Hadley Cantril conducted a study called *Invasion from Mars*, in which he analyzed the conditions that led to the audience's reaction and explained the behavior of those who witnessed it. The results revealed both the importance of the political context in which this insanity happened, and a series of other conclusions regarding the relationship between the public and the media: "the part played by the audience's trust in a particular media, the importance of the media content that was delivered, regardless of the context (the shape of a news bulletin and the voices of the experts added the trust is a real event), the importance of public predispositions ... issues of economic insecurity, translated into emotional insecurity" (P. Dobrescu, A. Bârgăoanu, 2003, p. 142). Following these conclusions, Paul Lazarsfeld and his collaborators edited the study

People's Choice where they explain that "new attitudes and modes of action come to the surface ... not only in extreme situations, but when a community is subjected to propaganda, when a significant event takes place or when an important decision must be made for the group" (P. Dobrescu, A. Bârgăoanu, 2003, pp. 142–143).

This opinion, corroborated with the fact that in his *Short History of Disinformation*, Vladimir Volkoff positions propaganda in the sphere of disinformation, leads to the conclusion that the media has all the necessary weapons to influence public opinion, whether by providing accurate information or disinformation. But for the influence to be achievable, we must first understand how media dependence is shaping up.

In this regard, we can take a look at the model of *uses and gratifications* proposed first by Paul Lazarsfeld and H. Hertzog and later developed by J. Blumler and Elihu Katz in 1974. "According to this orientation ... media consumption is an act of usage, depending on the expectations, needs and benefits involved; what media people *do* depends on what is expected of them; ... people select messages according to their image about the media; ... the media meet specific expectations, providing lower or higher user satisfaction; media consumption is the projection of industrial and collective expectations and the functional exigencies of social systems" (I. Dragan in M. Coman, p. 126).

Melvin DeFleur and Sandra Ball-Rokeach consider that in a developed society in which the media system is well established, the model of *uses and gratifications* is well defined, and the advantages thus obtained create true dependence on the media: "The more complex the society, the more comprehensive the range of personal purposes that require access to media information sources" (M.L. DeFleur, S. Ball-Rokeach, 1999, p. 305).

"People who have become addicted to television to reach a social understanding, for example, should select different types of television programs from people who depend on the audiovisual primarily for entertainment. If two people follow the same program, one for understanding and the other to have fun, they should receive different things and therefore be affected in different ways." (M.L. DeFleur, S. Ball-Rokeach, 1999, p. 308).

"In short, the media are understood as a system that controls limited and valuable resources, which give rise to interdependent relationships with other systems, relationships that produce cooperation motivated by a common interest, a conflict explainable by personal interests and a change to a more pronounced symmetry [which results in cooperation] or asymmetry of dependence [which results in conflict]." (M.L. DeFleur, S. Ball-Rokeach, 1999, p. 317).

In the first stage of the audience–media relationship, the public's dependence on the information transmitted by the communicators is created; subsequently, the process is carried out through which the receiver is subjected to persuasion exercised through the mass media – the second stage.

Regarding the influence of the media on the audience, Leo Bogart, quoted in *Introduction to the Media System,* says that "the media affect us deeply because they are a constant presence in our lives. Other institutions may have a stronger impact, but not one that is so persistent and profound … Besides, the media have a universality that no other institution has" (M. Coman, 1999, p. 106). Remy Rieffel adds that "From the moment the information is repeated … the cumulative minimal effects can trigger large-scale transformations" (M. Coman, 1999, p. 107).

Dennis McQuail also supports the previous idea, offering a classification of the categories on which the media acts: individuals, groups, institutions, the whole society, while it can also affect the human personality in its cognitive dimension, affective dimension or behavioral dimension (M. Coman, 1999, p. 106).

The specialized bibliography supports the hypothesis that the influence of the media can lead, in the case of individual receivers, to the achievement of *agreement, identification,* or *internalization of* values or meanings transmitted via the press.

- *The agreement* defines the conscious acceptance of the influence of a message; starting from the finding that there is a certain convergence between the opinions they have, and the values promoted by the respective message, the individual adheres, in a rational way, to its content. Adhesion is critical; it does not last and can be re-evaluated; it is conjectural and does not touch the deep structures of the personality of the individuals concerned.
- *Identification* involves assuming the values promoted *by* or *through* the media source and, consequently, imitating the behavior promoted by it. The identification processes are especially obvious in the field of

entertainment consumption. ... Facilitating identification, the creators of messages distributed through the media, try to attract and fix the public.
- *Internalization* involves the assimilation of values, meanings, and patterns of behavior disseminated by the media and their melting into the values that make up the individuals' view of the world and behaviors. This phenomenon achieves maximum effectiveness in the process of influencing. In general, internalization is the final point of an influencing process or, in more direct terms, of a persuasion campaign (M. Coman, 1999, p. 108).

Following this process of influencing as a result of the need induced by the media, the receiver comes into contact with that particular shape of information transmitted by journalists.

Jacques Legris, a journalist for the daily *Le Monde*, differentiates between the *objectivity of intention* (which "aims first to know the events, the facts, the people, the ideas, and then to make a judgment on them) and the *objectivity of appearance* which implies a judgment established beforehand, but avoids informing on it" (1976). Legris, quoted by Vladimir Volkoff, explains that *objectivity of intention* is difficult *to achieve* because of the processes it entails: "to practice inevitable sorting and amputations without falsifying too much perspective or proportion, seeking to fill gaps and illuminate dark areas with caution and rigor" (V. Volkoff, 1999, p. 166). Regarding the *objectivity of appearance*, Legris considers that this has the effect of clandestinely influencing the reader's consciousness, being about "programming, in a devious way, the selection that the reader will be determined to perform within the series of information transmitted to them daily, since they could neither read nor retain everything."

Legris lists several types of disinformation, applicable both in style and at the page and text level.

"In style, it will sometimes mean the introduction of a simple subordinate sentence, almost incidental, which will be enough to color the whole article ... It may also be the use of an ambiguous word, a double-meaning formula," procedures to which journalist Patrick Besson adds the *commas* saying that they "are in *Le Monde* what the French cancan is at the Moulin Rouge." Volkoff himself notes *interpretation* among the methods of exercising disinformation through the media: "an editorialist can be a disinformer; he is most often disinformed but, after taking a position on a certain situation, he will naturally try to prove that he was right, only to reveal the incidents that confirm his point of view;" the unequal parts by which genuine information will be allowed a narrower space than the one that disinforms; equal parts – after the public opinion adheres to the erroneous version, the publication claims its objectivity (1999, pp. 132, 134).

Page placement is also a good way to mislead the reader. A border note or a caricature placed next to a large article distracts from its contents or may change its original approach. Volkoff also mentions here the suspension points that indicate an interruption leading to the frustration of the reader. Eventually, "exact facts are reported, but alongside them is their rigged version, located almost on the same plane." The short paragraph, properly highlighted, representing the *informed* opinion of the editors, can involuntarily change the opinion of the receiver (V. Volkoff, 1999, p. 167).

Volkoff takes over a list of manipulations, drawn up by Legris, to which the journalistic text lends itself: "false symmetries, specious arguments presented as evidence; forgetting the past of some, recalling the past of others ... or, even more conveniently, crowded fillings, at the end of which the reader will rush to the final sentence, which will have the merit of being clear and deciding the conclusion that was to be imposed" (V. Volkoff, 1999, p. 167).

According to most authors, however, *visual representation* is the most powerful tool for disinforming the public. In practice, it is said that *an image is worth a thousand words* and that it can always replace a large part of the text or comment in the studio. Volkoff summarizes those traits on which the supremacy of the image resides:

- It is indisputable. We know that there are tricks or simply partial presentations, but some of us keep repeating that *we* have *to believe our eyes*.
- Visual information does not need to go through the brain to affect us. When you read about the *little girl full of blood* you are not as excited as when you *see* the *little girl full of blood*.
- The image, by its very nature, lends itself to all types of manipulation: selection, framing, filming angle, possible animation, all are

available to direct the viewer's attention to where the journalist wants and to whisper the interpretation that they have attributed to it.
- The image addresses the masses to a greater extent than words: it is easy to perceive, easy to reproduce, and immediately becomes the subject of conversation (V. Volkoff, 1999, pp. 176–177).

Given the fact that images are its raw materials, the author considers television a *paradise for the disinformer*. To support this claim, Volkoff provides the example of the breaking news that is placed at the opening of the news bulletin even if it is not of the utmost importance; increasing the number of news bulletins; the shortness of the interventions (maximum 120 seconds in the case of a report) to keep the audience connected (V. Volkoff, 1999, pp. 180, 181, 182). In this regard, journalist Jacques Merlino remembers an intercom command: "Tell me, Jacques, could you not give us an explanation of the Qur'an in 50 seconds?" and adds: "The chips are down, the public opinion is heated ... the reporter can only look for images that match the information already broadcast" (V. Volkoff, 1999, p. 182).

In support of what is written in *Short History of Disinformation,* Claude-Jean Bertrand introduces in the anthology *An Introduction to the Written and Audiovisual Press* some important blames which can be assigned to journalists in the process of circulating the press material:

- *Omissions*: the worst mistake of the press, because the reader finds it difficult to spot. This can be caused by lack of time or resources but also by the stingy owners or the journalists' lack of professionalism.
- The confusion between *entertainment* and *information* (a reality that led to the introduction of a hybrid term: *infotainment* based on the English words *information* and *entertainment*): the tendency to prioritize the sensational and make unpleasant journalistic materials *attractive*, to maintain a large audience.
- *News rather than information*: "the media is often content to make an absurd mosaic of obvious events, without cause and consequence. The user feels the need for landmarks, for reading guidelines."
- *The half-empty glass*: "good news is uninteresting" if it does not exploit the negative side of events and the sensational.
- *Incomprehensible information*: the inadequacy of language to the target audience's level of reception (2001, pp. 217–219).

The inaccuracies found in the press materials, that cause a slippage from the simple rendering of information, make the public blame the whole guild and contribute to the construction of the concept of *disinformation*. This reality is explained by a functionalist perspective associated with the media. "From such a perspective, the media as part of the social ensemble, respond to certain needs and consequently fulfill certain functions" (M. Coman, 1999, p. 72). "These functions vary according to the point of view of the media, of the whole society or only of the individual user; as the means of communication themselves or if the contents conveyed are taken into account; depending on what is examined: only their declared functions or also the hidden ones, only the positive or also the negative." (C.J. Bertrand, 2001, p. 34).

Theorists have highlighted various approaches to the main functions performed by the media. One of the best known is found in H. Lasswell's study, which includes the function of monitoring the environment, the correlation of different parts of society, and the transmission of traditions from one generation to another. A different approach is proposed by M. Mathien and acknowledged by Coman, who "opts for seven functions: evasion, social cohesion, distribution of knowledge, storage of current events, guide of current events, recreation, purification," (M. Coman, 1999, p. 73).

R.K. Merton made even more distinctions between *functions* (system-friendly consequences) and *dysfunctions* (unfavorable consequences), an idea also highlighted in the anthology *An Introduction to the Written and Audiovisual Press,* where C.J. Bertrand writes that "every function is affected by many dysfunctions." (2001, p. 36).

Next, we will review the most important functions performed by the media, as shown by most classifications, summarized by M. Coman in *Introduction to the Media System* (1999, p. 73–85), but also by C.J. Bertrand, who considers that the real functions of the press can be exercised only within the liberal model of the media that provides the necessary assumptions.

A. *The information function* is present, under one guise or another, in each classification, it is also mentioned in the chapter "Press Information" where we have dealt extensively with the issue of information and the needs of this function of the press American theorists call *supervision*. The expression emphasizes, in Coman's opinion, the status of the press as an instrument of reality control. "The role of the media is to obtain information and circulate it. And as information is found in abundance, the role of the media is to sort it, rank it, and interpret it. The press (written and audiovisual) is the one that indicates what is important and what is not in the array of events, processes, opinions, and personalities. The media decides whether or not to popularize new ideas" (C.J. Bertrand, 2001, p. 36).

B. The interpretation function. "A story is not just a sum of information items. A news item is a culturally determined view of the information. In other words, the content of a news item summarizes that information and the meanings assigned to it; journalistic texts provide both concrete data and meaning that can be attributed to the presented events or states. So, along with the facts, they also offer an interpretation of the same" (M. Coman, 1999, p. 77)

The first and (perhaps) most important form of interpretation is the very decision to make certain information public (or ignore it). The simple gesture of selecting a limited number of news items and reports from the clutter of data that daily assaults a newsroom involves both a value judgment and a process, not always perfectly conscious, of interpreting reality according to a set of norms, representations, symbols, and principles, etc. "It must be said that this first step is under the influence of the journalist's rationale, as their opinion will prevail, at least on an unconscious level; the choice is made according to the personal template of the mass-media employee."

"After this first filter, another stage of interpretation follows: setting priorities." At this stage, we identify those landmarks of great importance for the target audience, at least according to the journalists' opinions, i.e., the landmarks that will make up that day's *agenda*. "Thus, a small group of people sets a hierarchy of events, placing them at the top of newspaper pages or the beginning of radio and television news programs. This act, which has become a simple routine gesture, implies a deep social responsibility: if we accept the truth that more and more communities depend, for the knowledge of the world in which they live, on the information provided by the press and if we know that the hierarchies proposed by journalists influence public judgment [as also debated by Melvin DeFleur and Sandra Ball-Rokeach], then it is obvious that the choices and classifications offered by the media shape the social image of the *day*'s events, with its ups and downs, with priorities and areas of disengagement" (M. Coman, 1999, p. 77).

"Some means of communication play this role in particular: they provide the citizens with information and ideas from other places. They help the public acquire a global vision, giving them an increased social prestige" (C.J. Bertrand, 2001, p. 36). Bertrand calls this function the *presentation of an image of the world* and he joins it with the idea of *supervision*, thus creating a hybrid between the function of information and that of interpretation.

"If the selection and hierarchy of information are direct and implicit forms of interpretation, putting the news in context and commenting on it are direct, assumed forms of ascribing significance to events. In its beginnings, the press was dominated by the expression of opinions: magazines and newspapers were addressed to a cultured public, who wanted to debate various topics, to follow the struggle between interpretations, opinions, and counter-opinions on issues of major interest. ... The modern press, however, was built based on a convention, considered a golden rule by many researchers and journalists: the separation of the presentation of events from the personal opinions of those who present them" (M. Coman, 1999, p. 78). The one who synthesized this idea in 1992 was G.P. Scott, editor of *The Guardian*. He said that "the deeds are sacred; the comments are free." The rule is followed mostly in American and English journalism. As for the French press, Pierre Albert quoted by Coman considered that it "has always been more about expression than observation" (M. Coman, 1999, p. 79).

However, the interpretation process is not only about selection, ranking, and classification, but also about the ways of writing certain types of journalistic materials, known as *opinion articles*. Of these, the best known are the editorial and the commentary, but also the pamphlet, the chronicle, the caricature, etc.

The editorial is one of the indispensable materials in the written press, an article through which the publication can present its opinion about a certain problem, person, or event. The editorial is what often makes the biggest difference between dailies, being a distinctive element that gives personality to the newspaper.

Unlike the editorial, a *commentary* entails that a single person makes their opinion public and must be accountable for their published or disseminated opinions. A good example is that of Andy Rooney, a commentator for the CBS channel who, on his first day returning to work following a suspension, said: "Do we have opinions that can irritate certain people? You are right: we have such opinions. And that is why I am here, in front of you."

C. *The connection function.* "Every night, for half an hour, the television news magazine reviews the most important events of the day; however, the most important social fact, about which the news bulletin never speaks, is that at least half of the population of a country is immobilized, for half an hour, in front of the televised news" (J. Durand in M. Coman, 1999, p. 80).

"Indeed, by consuming media products, millions of people find themselves connected by countless unseen threads: being constantly exposed to the same messages, they end up sharing the same cultural values and representations, possessing similar knowledge, thinking through information, ideas, analogous stories, and symbols. Thus, no matter how different, an American, an African, or a European may find that they have the same moral judgments ..., that they know what happened in a particular country ... because they had the same sources of information from the media" (M. Coman, 1999, p. 80).

More than 30 years ago, American author Marshall McLuhan spoke, in his book *The Gutenberg Galaxy*, about a global village that would arise from the action of receiving information from the media, the dissemination of the same informative baggage and which is "dominated by a kind of spontaneous and unconscious solidarity, which he called *planetary tribalism*" (M. Coman, 1999, p. 80).

The solidarity mentioned above can be captured in the mass mobilizations that occurred as a result of mass messages related to certain issues of national interest, such as the floods in our country in 2005 and 2006, as well as movements at the continental or global level for saving whales or fighting breast cancer.

Mihai Coman considers that "thus, the press proves to be a builder of audiences, a maker of social networks, wider and more active, often, than the usual ones. Thanks to the press, people discover that they share the same values, that they can mobilize for the same purposes, in a word, that they are part of or can be part of a human community of infinitely more complex dimensions than those of the community in which they live and work every day" (M. Coman, 1999, p. 81). As a result, many theorists have concluded that one of the most important functions of the media, is to create an imaginary community – hence the term *glocalism*. A huge mass of relocated individuals who do not know each other, do not share the same values but have media consumption in common.

The link function is manifested, in the same way, at the society level, where unknown people interact having as a starting point a show they watch or a newspaper topic. Sociologists have analyzed this and concluded that the media manages to create a new form of solidarity specific to mass society.

Everyday reality has highlighted the dysfunctions of disseminating the same media content. This is manifest in the tendency to group and separate the masses based on their interpretation guidelines or on the public person whose opinion they share. This can lead to conflicts, but at the same time, the plurality of opinions is encouraged.

C.J. Bertrand calls the media link function *a forum for debate* and offers a special hypothesis that "the media forum plays a crucial political role" in making the connection between the rulers and the population. Hence the dysfunction that arises from the privilege of favoring a certain ideology against others or the promotion of the interests of certain groups (C.J. Bertrand, 2001, p. 38).

D. *The culturalization function.* "With the emergence and development of the media, a large part of the activities of transmitting cultural values and models, the formation of thinking and behavior were taken over by the press messages. At present, through the contents distributed by the media, the norms of generally accepted behavior, in other words, *the tacit conventions* of society are circulated and fixed. The press thus responds to the need of individuals and the community to perpetuate common values and to identify with those models that a community considers to be *landmarks of action*" (M. Coman, 1999, p. 82).

However, researchers concluded that the media propagate and support not only the healthy norms of society, but also deviant behaviors. Paul Lazarsfeld and R.K. Merton argue that "in the mass society, the function of publicly exposing a fact is institutionalized by the media. The press, radio, and television present to the public special antisocial facts and, in general, this presentation leads to a certain public action against what, perhaps, individually, would have been tolerated" (1972, p. 500).

The culturalization function that the media exercises is explicitly manifested through various specialized publications and shows. At a less obvious level, the media educates through productions in which patterns of behavior are inserted for members of society. The concept *of mass culture* was born precisely from these ways in which the media exerts its influence on the public and is closely related to McLuhan's *global village*, being both a determinant and a consequence of this expression. In the same way, valuable knowledge from various fields is transmitted to the next generations.

Lately, the guild of journalists has often been blamed for the fact that the function of educating the public has been neglected in favor of the entertainment that favors productions with an easy, relaxing content, which attracts the audience and has led to the birth of a society which G. Maffessoli called *hedonistic*.

E. *Entertainment function.* The episode "Who Shot J.R." from the *Dallas* series was watched in 1977 by 83 million viewers, while astronaut Neil Armstrong and his first steps on the moon aroused the interest of no less than 528 million people.

"In the mass society, entertainment is more necessary than ever to reduce the tensions that accumulate in each individual and that can lead to rebellion, illness or alienation. This entertainment is mainly offered by the media, thanks *to the mass cultures* they have created. Most consumers look for entertainment in the media. As a result, almost all the mass media offer it, even the dailies" (C.J. Bertrand, 2001, p. 38). The number and type of entertainment messages differ depending on the specifics of the medium and from one media institution to another.

Entertainment consumption does not only respond to the desire to relax and recover, after a tiring day; from another perspective, it helps people escape from the pressure of everyday life and find refuge in an imaginary world [the need for escapism]. Psychologists believe that through media products "people live *vicarious experiences*, benefiting, in an imaginary way, from feelings, events, and situations they could never live in real life." (M. Coman, 1999, p. 84). Jean Cazeneuve calls this feature of the media *a cathartic* or *therapeutic function,* referring to the fact that individuals find release from certain tensions or frustrations by assuming imaginary experiences and by projecting desires into the unreal worlds offered by the media.

The entertainment function "is the most important today, especially since it combines extremely efficiently with others. Education is received more easily when it is hidden under the guise of fun: television is much more efficient than school. Likewise, advertising tries to provide fun and seduce the audience, while even information is provided in the form of a show. By contrast, the media rarely offers pure entertainment; to entertain, they combine entertainment with another function" (C.J. Bertrand, 2001, p. 39).

"The essential problem is not that television gives us entertainment, but that it deals with all subjects in the form of entertainment ... This means that entertainment becomes the over-ideology of any television discourse" (N. Postman in M. Coman, 1999, p. 85).

We have achieved this development of the functions performed by the media starting from the assumption that the press takes on the role of responding to the different and constantly changing needs of the public. Thus, to be able to transmit "what is required," the mass media sometimes falls, intentionally or not, into the trap of broadcasting inaccuracies that often lead to misinformation.

But how do audiences react when they are bombarded with various media products. What do they select from the world they come in contact with? What do they manage or choose to retain from it?

Walter Lippmann and Jacques Ellul believe that public opinion is intrinsically linked to the presence and role of the media in contemporary society. In *Public Opinion*, the first study to deal exclusively with public opinion, Lippmann finds that the public perceives what they are prepared to perceive. They meet a multitude of new facts and situations with certain knowledge, with a cultural and experience background, often condensed into stereotypes of an intellectual nature, through which they regard and try to understand reality (P. Dobrescu, A. Bârgăoanu, 2003, p. 50).

Moreover, Lippmann considers that the mass opinion has some typical errors of assessment. First, its reaction is slower than the reality to which it refers. Mass opinions are par excellence inertial, because "it takes more time to change more minds than a few." Inertial reactions are more obvious when new situations arise that need new approaches, new analyses, and new situations. Under the pressure of events, the opinion eventually changes, only in the meantime the situation itself may have changed. Only after it is set in motion can the mass opinion discover that "it relates to a situation that no longer exists" (W. Lippmann in P. Dobrescu, A. Bârgăoanu, 2003, p. 50).

In conclusion, the public itself can be a driver of disinformation. Any information that is independent or processed in a media product passes through the filter of public opinion that can detect the elements of incoherence or can, just as easily, distort it.

CHAPTER III: Manipulation

III.1. Overview

The word *manipulation* (lat. *manipulatio*) is as often used as it is ambiguous. Journalists and politicians often abuse it. Even some social science researchers give it meaning which is, if not wrong, at least lacking in specificity. For example, French psychosociologist Alex Mucchielli (2000, p. 191) thinks that 'influence, persuasion, propaganda, manipulation,' etc. are the same. Another example: Bogdan Ficeac who refers indiscriminately to propaganda, hypnosis, brainwashing, neurolinguistic communication, etc., emcompassing them all into the concept of *manipulation* (Septimiu Chelcea, 2006, p. 225).

However, Chelcea also mentions certain attempts to establish the scope of the concept. One of these materializes in the study *La Manipulation politique,* written by Pierre Lenain and published in 1985. Advocating a theory of manipulation, the French political scientist says: "All societies have an important part of manipulation: the relationship *(trust)* between government and those governed is necessarily the object of manipulation, no government can be disinterested in controlling opinion, trying to influence it, to shape it, to orient it, to *form it*; whether manipulation is short-term or long-term, politics involves intervening on the political imaginary of the partisans, using fictions, illusions, special rhetoric, half-truths, concealment, slander, rumor, traps; the political circumstances are woven by thousands of heterogeneous actions, the majority and the opposition each playing a complex game, which deviates perfectly from the right path" (S. Chelcea, 2006, p. 225).

Manipulation, the quoted author believes, "is an everyday fact, a privileged instrument of political art, through which power strengthens its position, and the opposition tries to change the balance of power" (S. Chelcea, 2006, p. 226).

We believe that the elements captured above by Pierre Lenain also paint the relationship between the media and its audiences, therefore, the theory is applicable in this case as well.

In the *Explanatory Dictionary of Journalism, Public Relations and Communication*, the term *manipulation* appears defined as an "altered form of communication using in variable doses biased argumentation, lying, information which is truncated, arranged, staged, including through a test balloon. Rumor, diversion – in the vicinity (or in the service) of propaganda, (so in the vicinity of using persuasion), taking the form of public relations – mainly publicity – which seeks to create erroneous opinions in an individual, group, or class. It is based on incorrect information about attitudes, actions contrary to their interests. A *manipulation* is a form of deception" (2002, p. 210).

Septimiu Chelcea also defines the concept that he observes in its dynamic form and emphasizes the purpose of exercising this dynamic, that of achieving a *change* in perceptions of any kind. "The term *manipulation* refers to the action of changing opinions, attitudes, and behaviors by exposing people and human groups to messages to achieve goals desired by someone else (individuals or organizations) without applying physical constraints and without awareness of the discrepancy between people and target groups' distant goals and the distant goals of those who exercise influence" (2006, p. 226).

Chelcea also says that "unlike persuasion, which may or may not be condemnable depending on the purpose of influence, manipulation is always subject to moral and/or legal sanctions" (S. Chelcea, 2006, p. 226). "Manipulated people are not encouraged to think about the situation, but are lured by false promises, deceived by verbal or nonverbal behaviors, or are *maneuvered*, in the sense that the fabricated situation limits their choices. Manipulation differs from persuasion in that it does not directly urge thinking together with others. Through deceptive tactics, individuals are guided to do, by free consent, what the person who persuades them has chosen" (K.K. Reardon in S. Chelcea, 2006, p. 225).

"In the case of manipulation, the following defining notes should be kept in mind: influencing opinions, attitudes, and behaviors (OAB); exposure to messages; the aim is to achieve goals other than those of the manipulated persons; there is a discrepancy, sometimes even an opposition, between the distant goals of those who manipulate and those who are manipulated; the target persons and groups are not aware of the existence of that discrepancy or opposition; those who manipulate do not use physical coercion to achieve their goals" (S. Chelcea, 2006, p. 227).

The same author makes a clear distinction between manipulation and other forms of influence such as persuasion, propaganda, and advertising.

Characteristics of manipulation, persuasion, advertising, and propaganda.

Characteristics	Manipulation	Persuasion	Advertising	Propaganda
Changing the OAB	+	+	+	+
Exposure to messages	+	+	+	+
No constraint	+	+	+	+ -
Target people aware of the goal	-	+	+ -	+ -
Rational process	-	+ -	- +	+ -
Opposite goals	+	- +	- +	- +
Public character	+ -	+ -	+	+
Profitable	- +	- +	+	+ -
Negative consequences for the individual	+	- +	- +	+ -
Negative consequences for society	+	+ -	-	+ -

"Manipulation and persuasion are two psychological processes whose characteristics are close (out of ten, five characteristics are common), but which are ethically different; advertising and propaganda are two similar social activities (out of ten, four characteristics are common), but applicable in different sectors of social life.

Persuasion or manipulation can be used in advertising and propaganda activities, either separately or at the same time as ways of changing opinions, attitudes and behaviors. By *behavioral manipulation* we understand the influencing of human subjects to *perform* actions which come against their own goals, without them – the human subjects – being aware of the discrepancy between their own goals and the distant goals of those who influence them" (S. Chelcea, 2006, p. 227).

Behavioral manipulation is also a topic addressed in several ways by French researchers Robert-Vincent Joule and Jean-Léon Beauvois in the *Treatise on Manipulation*. The two psychology professors propose a typology of methods in which an individual can be determined to act contrary to their own beliefs. This approach is based on events involving ordinary people but also examples of cases of manipulation studied by scientists in certain contexts. The whole study starts from the assumption that "to get someone to adopt a behavior that they would have preferred not to follow – and that they would not have been expected to at a simple direct request – by calling things, this means *manipulation*" (1997, p. 7). In the "Introduction," the authors present the following opinion: "In fact, there are only two effective ways to obtain the behavior we want from someone: the exercise of power (or power relations) and manipulation" (R.V. Joule, J.L. Beauvois, 1997, p. 7).

Joule and Beauvois connect *behavioral manipulation* with the *manipulation of morality,* a process that is found in everyday life and which, according to the two, can be most easily identified in business relationships. The presented example starts from the idea that "the determination of a first behavior in controlled conditions aiming to obtain others, means manipulation" (R.V. Joule, J.L. Beauvois, 1997, p. 144). Thus, the customer who buys a certain product "has been put in a position which is not that of the *free* and *responsible* individual that morals and the official economy preach. He is *de facto* placed in the position of an economic being who can only be: a buyer without moods whose consumer image appears after the revelation of their buying behaviors," (R.V. Joule, J.L. Beauvois, 1997, p. 144). In this case, "morals are a little crowded in a corner" because the sales technique used (manipulation through advertising) does not serve the interest or desires of the customer, but those of the trader who seeks to make a profit.

Septimiu Chelcea considers that behavioral manipulation is based on conformity – the change of a person's position in the direction of the group's position – and obedience – the change of a person's behavior as a result of an order given by a legitimate authority.

However, Joule and Beauvois emphasize the effectiveness of the so-called *illusion of freedom* that affects the manipulated in the form of the *feeling of freedom,* a determining factor for the individual to keep their original *commitment.* "It is not uncommon to see manipulators directing people to the analysis of what they believe or feel deeply, doing so voluntarily, or more plausibly, involuntarily, in a behavioral setting that ultimately ensures the effectiveness of their actions. We will not risk the hypothesis that this focus on the analysis of beliefs and feelings has as its sole purpose diversion and turning the individual's attention from the thousands of ridiculous behaviors that we extort from them and that may be enough to give rise to less ridiculous acts than someone would expect" (1997, p. 68).

In his study, *Manipulation Techniques,* Bogdan Ficeac offers another perspective on behavior and opinion manipulations. This angle excludes all free will or the feeling of freedom and proposes a different kind of control over the individual. "*Total control* over the individual means total control over *their way of thinking, their behavior* and *their feelings.* Totalitarian systems pursuing unconditional obedience of the people focus on creating a kind of citizen who is *unable to make decisions alone.*

Consequently, the essence of total control over the individual lies in the annihilation of their feeling of independence, a feeling that could make them think, create their system of values and make decisions on their own" (2004, p. 125). It is obvious that such situations are not normally found in a democratic society, but some principles seem to be applicable, in an adapted form, to certain areas of non-totalitarian societies. "To put total control over people's minds, they must be immersed in the anonymity of the maneuvered masses, be permanently dependent on the thinking system of the group they belong to and submit unconditionally, instinctively to the authorities" (B. Ficeac, 2004, p. 125).

The author showcases the so-called method *of brainwashing,* a technique used in the beginning during the Korean War, and through which American prisoners "were subjected to an intensive treatment of manipulation of thought, as a result of which they came to serve the pro-Korean propaganda., against the interests of the United States" (B. Ficeac, 2004, p. 125). From an empirical perspective, in contemporary society, this term has come to be related to the effect that the media can have on the minds and thinking of audiences. Thus, the words approached the meaning of the term 'manipulation.'

Next, Bogdan Ficeac introduces a necessary factor for the emergence of manipulation of any kind. He says that "in terms of social psychology, we can speak of manipulation when a certain social situation is created *premeditatedly* to influence the relationships and behavior of manipulated people in the sense desired by the manipulator" (2004, p. 30).

Ficeac is also the one who proposes a classification of manipulations. In this sense, he uses as a criterion the amplitude of changes made in a particular social situation, citing Philip Zimbardo, a professor at Stanford University in California. "It should be noted here that, although in this sense the manipulations can be classified as small, medium-sized, and large, their consequences do not follow a strict correspondence with the amplitude of the initial changes. For example, small changes can have major consequences and vice versa" (B. Ficeac, 2004, p. 30).

"*Small manipulations,* obtained through minor changes in the social situation, can sometimes have surprisingly large effects. For example, donations can increase significantly when the request is accompanied by a small, seemingly insignificant service, an appeal to heavenly blessing, or even just the image of the person making the request. ... Beggars also use countless tricks to stimulate the charitable spirit of the passers-by" – shabby appearance, very young children, physical mutilation but also certain words that have the role of raising awareness. (B. Ficeac, 2004, p. 31).

"*Medium-sized manipulations* refer to important changes in social situations, with effects that sometimes dramatically exceed expectations, precisely because the enormous power of influencing social situations on human behavior is underestimated in most cases" (B. Ficeac, 2004, p. 35). Ficeac uses the case of the Romanian revolution of 1989 to highlight his approach. He observes that "besides the techniques meant to induce the feeling of submission to the authorities or, on the contrary, to trigger strong revolts, other examples of average manipulations can be those aimed at dehumanizing the victims or deindividualizing the attackers, to encourage the aggressive spirit. ... In concrete terms, the methods used in the propaganda aimed at dehumanizing the enemy consist in imposing through the media horrible caricatures, aggressive slogans, and falsified press materials, in which the enemies are presented as violent and dangerous troglodytes." (B. Ficeac, 2004, p. 41).

"*Large manipulations* come with the influence of the whole culture in the middle of which the individual lives. The value system, the behavior, the way of thinking of the individual are determined first of all by the written and unwritten norms of the society in which they live, by the subcultures with which they come in contact. By neglecting this permanent and huge influence, the individual can make misjudgments much easier or can be easily manipulated. At the same time, it should be noted that, precisely due to the continuous action of large manipulations on us, their presence has become something common, being much more difficult to identify" (B. Ficeac, *2004,* p. 43).

The example invoked by Bogdan Ficeac and proposed, initially, by the Swiss psychologist Jean Piaget, is that of *the education system.* The school is, in most cases, the environment that gives the child both the knowledge and conduct necessary for the future adult. In this sense, the student acquires the *spirit of subordination to the authorities,* acquires a *sense of responsibility,* understands the need and gets used to a *fixed program,* develops and acquires the *spirit of competition.* In the context of a totalitarian system, all these are adapted to create a deindividualized and submissive character. However, the idea can be extrapolated to democratic societies in which "major manipulations underlie the spread of different currents of opinion, form traditions, and customs, outline mentalities, determine *fashionable* currents or even lead to large protests." (B Ficeac, 2004, p. 45).

III.2. Short Classification of Manipulations

Septimiu Chelcea supports the hypothesis proposed by Jean-Léon Beauvois and Robert Vincent Joule who considered that "for a change of attitude it is more efficient to obtain a preparatory behavior than persuasion. In this sense, psychosociological strategies (sometimes called techniques) of pressure-free submission (manipulation) can be used" (S. Chelcea, 2006, p. 232). Among them, some stand out: *foot-in-the-door, door-in-the-face,* and *low-ball* or *priming* joined by *contextualizing the situation, compliance, information about the majority opinion, going around the table, default self-fulfilling prophecy.*

- *Foot-in-the-door,* as a decision-making strategy, was proposed, analyzed, and experimentally verified by Jonathan L. Freedman and Scott C. Fraser in the mid-1970s. The principle is this: ask for a little, so that, in the end, you get what you wanted. Numerous situations in everyday social life, as well as experiments designed by psychosociologists, verify the principle on which this manipulation technique is based. An intimate relationship often begins with an innocent touch of the hand. ... If they agreed with the political platform of a party, most people also participate in political actions (rallies, marches, donations, etc.) in favor of that party (S. Chelcea, 2006, p. 233). The studies carried out by the two researchers were based, in particular, on experiments using the *classic foot-in-the-door procedure,* which Joule and Beauvois describe as follows: "a non-problematic and inexpensive preparatory behavior is obtained from the subject, obviously, in a framework of free choice and in circumstances that facilitate engagement. ... The foot-in-the-door effect is an effect of perseverance in upholding a previous decision, the subjects engaged in a first freely decided behavior accepting more easily a subsequent application that follows the same course, although much more expensive" (1997, p. 74). The *Manipulation Treaty* also mentions the manipulation technique called *foot-in-the-door with implicit demand,* which is considered to have an advantage: "if in the classical version, the individual's suspicion can be aroused by the succession of the two demands and, consequently, of two events, in the technique with implicit demand it is no longer the case since the second event appears as purely coincidental" (R.V. Joule, J.L. Beauvois, 1997, p. 87).
- The technique called *door-in-the-face* was first included in the study *A Reciprocal Concession Procedure for Inducing Compliance: The Door-In-The-Face Technique,* published in 1975 by Robert B. Cialdini et al. The results of several experiments were commented on in the study. This manipulation technique is based on the principle that you have to ask for more from the beginning, to get less, exactly as much as you need (S. Chelcea, 2006, p. 235). "If we start by asking someone for an extreme favor, the refusal of which is certain, and if we then move to lower this demand, the individual could feel a normative pressure to respond to our concession through their concession. If the situation is

such that the other's response to our request fatally involves a dichotomous choice — yes or no — the only way for them to demonstrate reciprocity is to move from the initial position of rejection to a position of acceptance. Thus, by an indirect means of illusory withdrawal from the initial position, it is possible to determine the other to accept the request we wanted them to accept from the beginning" (Cialdini et al., 1975, p. 207).

- *The low-ball* is a psychosociological behavior handling technique and has a relatively recent scientific status. The concept was finalized and demonstrated by Robert B. Cialdini and his collaborators in 1978, often being used by *persuasion specialists* (merchants, teachers, priests, doctors, etc.). The principle underlying this technique is the following: obtaining the decision for action from a person without them knowing the real cost of the action or with them counting on a fictitious advantage. Despite subsequent information, people tend to maintain their initial decisions (S. Chelcea, 2006, p. 238). "Low-ball means revealing the hidden costs of the action after the subject has decided to act," (Ștefan Boncu, 2002, p. 387). "The low-ball technique supports the saying: *Where the thousand went, the hundred goes, too!* Sometimes, being manipulated, people seem to follow an even more damaging principle: *Where a hundred went, a thousand goes, too!"* (S. Chelcea, 2006, p. 241).

- *Contextualizing the situation* is also a recent technique that is based on the transition from simplistic sender-receiver communication to the psychosociological understanding of the process. According to A. Mucchielli, "communication is no longer seen as the transmission of a message, but rather as a construction of meaning that things acquire for people" (2002, p. 39). "The true art of manipulation – and therefore of influence and persuasion – consists in disguised work on the invisible behaviors of the situation" (2002, p. 54).

- *Information about the majority opinion.* This manipulation technique is based on the individual's fear of being excluded if they display a different opinion than the majority. *The spiral of silence,* one of the strong effects of the media on public opinion, is a consequence of this process of manipulation. Thus, the individual prefers not to express their point of view in order not to risk being in conflict with an opinion which the majority considers correct.

- *Going around the table* is a manipulation technique that, following an experiment led by Solomon E. Asch, can be explained as follows: if the organizers of a meeting try to obtain the agreement of the participants on a certain problem and they make it so that "by chance" the first three or four speeches support the point of view of the organizers, it is most likely that the other participants will decide in the same direction, will support positions that they do not hold because they wish to align with the opinion considered *fair* (S. Chelcea, 2006, p. 259).
- *Implicit self-fulfilling prophecy.* This expression belongs to the American sociologist Robert K. Merton who published a study with the same name, based on the following theorem: if a person defines situations as real, then they are real in their consequences. In essence, from false premises, true conclusions are drawn.
- *Compliance* or the act of making people agree without thinking in advance is based on six principles formulated by Robert B. Cialdini: reciprocity, consistency, social proof, authority, sympathy, rarity. Septimiu Chelcea believes that "their implementation in different fields of social life (trade, education, politics, etc.) can have beneficial results for the person who submits to a request, an exhortation, an advice or, on the contrary, can be harmful, as is the case of manipulation" (2006, p. 243). Cialdini illustrates compliance with the *Turkey hen and her chicks* and the *Autopilot*. The first of the two suggests that decisions of any kind of individuals are hereditary predetermined, while the second considers that reason has a central role in controlling behavior but does not deny the force of innate impulses (2006, pp. 243, 244).
  * *Compliance* is well illustrated, as a manipulation technique, through *nonverbal* communication. Thus, when a politician or any other opinion leader addresses the masses, they must demonstrate the similarities between them and their listeners. These similarities are reflected in clothing, vocabulary, manner of address, etc. "Many people cannot separate the substance of the message from the author of the message. This is all the more true in the case of speakers' persuasion, when the speaker's attitudes, voice and appearance constantly interact with what they say" (H.W. Simons in S. Chelcea, 2006, p. 270).

1. The *principle of reciprocity* generates, according to Septimiu Chelcea, "the most widespread manipulation technique, given that the rule of reciprocity is found with all peoples and at all times" (2006, p. 244). American sociologist Alvin Gouldner considered reciprocity *the golden rule* in interpersonal relationships in all societies. However, Robert Cialdini quoted by Chelcea draws attention to the fact that the rule of reciprocity may not always develop fair exchanges, but also dishonest exchanges, and can be exploited for profit. The same author explains the mechanism of this principle: "the rule of reciprocity imposes reciprocal concessions in two ways: on the one hand, it pressures the person to whom a concession was made to respond in the same way, on the other hand, it ensures the person initiating the concession (help, favor, gift) that it will not be exploited. And yet, initiating a concession can be part of a *door-in-the-face* manipulation technique," (2006, p. 244).
2. The *principle of commitment and consistency* causes us to behave in the same way now and in the future as we did in the past. "Let's be predictable," S. Chelcea explains. About this principle, Cialdini is quoted in S. Chelcea's book saying that "the need to be (and seem) consistent, is a very strong means of social influence, often leading to actions in ways that are clearly opposed to our interests" (2006, p. 244).
3. The *principle of social proof* states that spontaneously we consider that a behavior is correct (including our own behavior) if we perceive that others proceed in the same way and obtain the desired results. "Social proof," says Robert B. Cialdini, "provides *a* convenient *shortcut* to establish how to behave at a given time, but at the same time makes the person who uses it vulnerable to the attacks of profiteers waiting along the road" (2004, p. 149). Chelcea offers the following example: "the practice of broadcasting laughs recorded on tape during TV programs is an example of the application of the principle of social proof. If so many people laugh heartily, you laugh too! The joke is good – we are *obliged* to accept, whether we like it or not" (2006, p. 248).
4. The *principle of sympathy*. To mirror this theory, Chelcea offers some tricks that have the role of influencing or even manipulating.
    - The effect of similarity – often our automatic response is positive if the request is made by someone who is like us in terms of physical or psycho-moral characteristics;
    - The effect of proximity – spatial proximity conditions psychological closeness (sympathy);

- The effect of physical beauty – Aristotle said that "beauty is stronger than any letter of recommendation." Regarding the consequence of this fact, Cialdini says that: "People with a pleasant physical appearance enjoy an enormous social advantage in our culture. They are more likable, more convincing, are helped more often, and are perceived as having better character traits and superior intellectual abilities" (2006, p. 250).
- The effect of compliments – people want to be complimented and tend to sympathize with others praising them;
- The effect of association – A.M. Lee and E.B. Lee, pioneers of the analysis of persuasion and manipulation techniques, came to the conclusion that a transfer occurs when associating a desired thing or a person invested with prestige with other things or people. There is a phenomenon of *admiration by association.*
- The effect of coupling politics with food – over time, it has been observed that politicians, in particular, tend to associate food pleasures with the ideas, processes, and people present at the table. The demonstration of this effect has its origin in the experiments of Russian scientist Ivan P. Pavlov. He showed how conditioned reflexes arise. If an object repeatedly appears in association with something that elicits a favorable or unfavorable response, that object will determine the same favorable or unfavorable response.

5. The *principle of authority* – starting from the premise that individuals tend to submit to the authority of any kind, Robert B. Cialdini mentioned in *Psychology of Persuasion* some ways to use the *principle of authority* to manipulate (S. Chelcea, 253–255):
   - Academic titles – this one almost automatically triggers the acceptance of the statements coming from the bearers of the epistemic authority, of the expert, and the following of their advice and exhortations without hesitation.
   - Clothes of authority – in general, clothing is a marker of class and social power, as well as professional categories. Cialdini says that "*scam artists* change their clothes like chameleons; they adopt the white of hospitals, the black of priests, the green of the army or the blue of the police, as the situation demands, to obtain maximum

advantage. Their victims realize too late that the clothes of authority cannot be a guarantee at all."
- Luxury cars – a study showed that, at least in traffic, Americans show more consideration to drivers of luxury cars compared to those who drive economy class cars.
6. The *principle of rarity* – according to these theories, people, objects, or occasions seem all the more valuable the less available they are. "Everything that is rare or becomes rare will be more valuable" (R.B. Cialdini in S. Chelcea, 2006, p. 255).

The above-listed principles of *compliance* do not act independently but in conjunction. Thus, those who want to manipulate us combine the principle of sympathy and that of rarity, the principle of social proof, reciprocity and academic titles, etc.

In general, manipulation cannot be considered the prerogative of a certain segment of society or a social class. Different types of manipulation are common in everyday life, in a multitude of contexts. Interpersonal relationships, the rules by which any community operates, feelings of friendship, the desire to belong to certain groups, or seemingly unimportant gestures are often the prerequisites for manipulation. Many of these sometimes remain unconscious, the individual not being able to perceive them or treating them as small compromises necessary in the process of adaptation.

In his book, *Manipulation Techniques,* Bogdan Ficeac introduced the chapter entitled "Twenty-two practical tips to resist manipulation." *The* ideas presented here intend to familiarize the individual with the reality of everyday manipulation and lead them to sanction such attempts. These things happen, according to R.V. Joule and J.L. Beauvois, because "not everyone has enough power, or the pressure means to get what they want from another. ... Does that mean that the vast majority of people do not expect anything from anyone? No, of course not. Most of the time, we expect a certain behavior (advantageous for us!) from people over whom we have neither power nor means of pressure" (1997, p. 8).

Consequently, as a general rule of counterattack, we suggest advice number 19, proposed by B. Ficeac: "Act consciously in all situations. Don't make decisions just because you have to or because you are conditioned to. Try to see which reflexes correspond to your intimate beliefs and which have been imposed on you by various manipulation techniques" (2004, p. 219).

"On the life stage, each of us would like to write their role and interpret their destiny in such a way as to reach an end according to their desires. But because we are social beings, monologue is not a solution. We must choose our lines so that they fit into a particular choir. Sometimes, or even oftentimes, it is very possible that the lines we imagine are dissonant or not accepted by other actors. That is why a director is needed to take on the role of reconciling all personal roles. By obeying him, we lose our autonomy and integrate into the system. ... We no longer know where the role we wrote for ourselves ends and where the ones written by others begin. We can't tell who, why, and when wrote the script that tells us what to think, what to do, what to feel. And it often happens that a Director goes beyond the simple condition of dispatcher ... and begins to believe himself a demiurge, to see the others as simple extras in a play written by him, for him; to them, this play is foreign. In such cases, sooner or later, the plays turn into horrible tragedies" (B. Ficeac, 2004, p. 5).

In a society that Bernard Miege characterized as being *conquered by communication*, the media is often confused with that Director about whom Bogdan Ficeac speaks. The press of any kind seems to dictate the public agenda with its priorities and points of interest. The press represents the mass media outlets, the channels through which those who take part in events or even the artisans of the news, the real Directors, transmit their messages to the audiences they target, to achieve their objectives.

III.3. Manipulation through the Media

In the *Explanatory Dictionary of Journalism, Public Relations and Communication*, the term *manipulation* appears defined as an "altered form of communication using in variable doses biased argumentation, lying, information which is truncated, arranged, staged, including through a test balloon. Rumor, diversion – in the vicinity (or in the service) of propaganda, (so in the vicinity of using persuasion), taking the form of public relations – mainly publicity – which seeks to create erroneous opinions in an individual, group, or class. It is based on incorrect information about attitudes, actions contrary to their interests. *A manipulation* is a form of deception" (C.F. Popescu, 2002, p. 210).

Regarding the *manipulation of information,* Jean Cazeneuve said that it "succeeds if propaganda is presented as information and information as objective. Biased information can fabricate opinion through a series of procedures: selecting information, amputating information, transforming context ..., by amalgamating pieces of information with others that have nothing to do with them but disqualify them ... emphasizing what is secondary to the detriment of the essential, disseminating fake news" (1970, p. 270).

Unlike the classifications mentioned in the previous subchapter, the manipulation of public opinion is now under discussion, because it is "the key to any act of manipulation through the press. Those who initiate the acts of manipulation aim to change the media in their favor" (Sonia C. Stan, 2004, p. 17). Plato said that "opinion means speaking, and opinion consists in an explicit discourse."

About *public opinion,* Edward L. Bernays considers that "it is the term that defines a diffuse, unstable and changing group of individual judgments. Public opinion is the aggregated result of the individual opinions – sometimes consensual, sometimes conflicting – of the people who make up a society or any social group. ... The thinking of the ordinary man consists of a mass of judgments on most subjects that come into contact with his psychological and mental life" (2003, p. 74). Septimiu Chelcea analyzes the phrase in detail and dedicates a large part of the study called *Public Opinion: Persuasion and Manipulation Strategies* to the relationship between public opinion and the media: "Mass communication can activate latent attitudes and, through this, the emergence of individual opinions. The sharing of those opinions marks the beginning of the gradual process of transforming individual opinions into public opinion" (2006, p. 87).

Research has concluded that the impact of the media on public opinion is crucial, while some surveys have shown that the influence is minimal. In any case, the connection between the two entities has never been disputed. And most studies have revealed the idea that the media contributes to 1) the crystallization of individual and group opinions; 2) building currents of opinion; 3) mediation between public opinion and government; 4) change of public opinion (Ion Dragan, 1996, p. 170).

Among those who analyzed the forms of influence attributed to the media are Melvin De Fleur, Sandra Ball-Rokeach, D. McQuail, W.J. Severin and J.W. Tankard jr., Ion Dragan, John Fiske, or Fr. Balle. The theories of effects were divided into three categories: strong, limited, and weak. Next, we will review the classes of strong and weak effects – considered relevant for this chapter, as presented in *Introduction to the Media System* (1999, pp. 109–124), considering that they highlight the clearest form of influence exerted by the press on the audience.

- The *stimulus-response* model which appeared in the 1980s and is also called *the one-step flow* or *hypodermic needle theory* is based on the idea that messages reach the receiver directly, not being filtered by any social (individual, group, organization, etc.) or cultural (traditions, symbolic systems, view of the world) factor. According to this interpretation, as soon as the message reaches the receiver, it triggers a uniform reaction – just as an external stimulus triggers spontaneous sensory reactions in the human body. The name hypodermic needle metaphorically emphasizes the following two ideas: a) the press messages penetrate the recipient's consciousness with the ease of a needle piercing the skin; b) they generate an immediate, fast, and uncontrolled rational response, analogous to the one provoked by a stab. Along the same lines, the same vein, the *magic bullet* – a phrase attributed to M. De Fleur and S. Ball-Rokeach, seems to be an *enchanted* tool that shapes public opinion. For this model to work, the two authors believe that "individuals should find themselves in situations of psychological isolation, to maintain impersonal relationships of interaction with their peers and to be broken by informal social ties and obligations" (1999, p. 157). The *magic bullet* theory "appears as a mechanistic model and lacks the subtlety of explaining the relationship between the press and the audience, a model that considers that the media directly inject values, ideas and information into passive individuals (who are part of an atomized audience), producing a direct and immediate effect" (T. O'Sullivan in M. Coman, 1999, p. 110). Because of this, the model is outdated, with limited possibilities for applicability, such as crises.

* The scheme pertaining to the *stimulus-response* model is as follows:

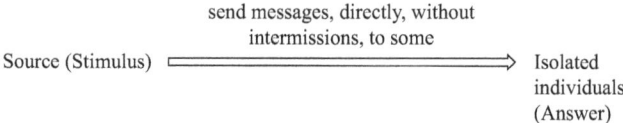

(M. Coman, 1999, p. 110)

- The *hegemonic* model was supported, in particular, by researchers grouped around the Birmingham School but also by representatives of current cultural studies such as J. Fiske, J. Lull, St. Hall. According to these theories, the ruling classes express their power, in moments of economic and social stability, not so much through repressive measures, but symbolic persuasive means. Thus, using the educational system and the mass information channels, they impose their ideology in the form of general, neutral, and universally valid truths. The media thus becomes the instrument of hegemonic tendencies promoted by those in power, imposing the interests of a class. Like the previous model, the hegemonic theory presupposes the existence of a passive, strongly receptive public. In the case of a critical audience, the information would no longer be assimilated automatically, even in the conditions of modern society's dependence on the media.
- The *addiction* model was introduced in 1976 by Melvin De Fleur and Sandra Ball-Rokeach who argue that "political, economic or other systems in modern societies depend on the media to establish communication relationships. In other words, the press controls the information and communication resources that other systems need to function efficiently" (1999, p. 236). The two authors consider that the relations between the media and the other systems give the measure of the individuals' dependence on the mass media. The relationship transforms from a bilateral press/individual one, into a relationship with three actors: press/social institutions/individual. Mihai Coman deduces from this the fact that the power of the press decreases when the mediating entities are strong and increases when they are weak. "When the press remains the only system for distributing information, the potential of media messages to have

various cognitive, emotional or behavioral effects increases" (M. De Fleur, S. Ball-Rockeach, 1999, p. 242–243). The more developed societies are and the greater the degree of urbanization, the more dependent individuals become on the information provided by the media because they cannot have access to interpersonal or institutional communication channels.

The *spiral of silence* model is the theory proposed by German researcher Elisabeth Noelle-Neumann and is based on five premises: a) people are afraid of isolation, they want to be received and integrated into the communities around them; b) society tends to marginalize individuals who have deviant behaviors or who have different values from those accepted by most of its members; c) the fear of isolation urges people to constantly evaluate the state, directions, fluctuations of common opinions; d) these evaluations affect the public reactions of individuals, as they constantly try to comply with the general collective line of behavior and thinking; e) based on these processes of adapting to the mass and giving up the dissonant elements, a majority public opinion is created and maintained. To these, Ion Dragan quoted by Coman adds the idea that "the media is the main reference element in expressing and distributing opinions. Press messages are conceived as a kind of witness to the distribution of legitimate opinions, being used by individuals as selective indicators to determine who is entitled to speak publicly (legitimate opinions) and who should remain silent. The media, more precisely the communicators (journalists), are the ones who have the power to decide and define what is important and legitimate in judging different events or elements of public life" (1999, p. 115).

According to E. Noelle-Neumann, the power of the media to impose a certain opinion can result in two phenomena:

1. the creation of a silent minority: groups that are not found in the media discourse represent isolated segments and their *silence* does not affect the general movement of society but by ignoring them, the media leaves in the background its democratic responsibility.
2. creating a silent majority: the media most often expresses views that do not belong to the masses but to leaders or even journalists, causing large

groups to slip into the spiral of silence. However, their opinion becomes visible during events that guarantee anonymity, such as voting. In conclusion, the spiral of silence model states that "when controversial issues are being debated, the direction that public opinion follows ... is decisively shaped by the press" (E. Noelle-Neumann in M. Coman, 1999, pp. 115–116).

With the deepening of research on the influence of the media on its audiences, less radical conclusions were reached, which gave rise to *theories of limited effects,* shaped by Bernard Berelson and taken up in the *Introduction to the media*: "Certain types of communication, referring to certain problems, brought to the attention of certain categories of public, under certain conditions, can produce certain effects" (M. Coman, 1999, p. 116). This new approach will focus on the elements that mediate the relationship between media messages and reception processes, as well as on the selective nature of acceptance and assimilation of media content.

The *two-step flow* first appeared in the study called *People's Choices,* published in 1944 by P. Lazarsfeld, B. Berelson, and H. Gaudet. This work analyzed the citizens' voting behavior. Later, the theory was addressed in other research such as *Personal Influence,* written by Elihu Katz and Paul Lazarsfeld.

"This new model marks a change of perspective. Individuals are no longer seen as uniform and isolated entities; they enter into interpersonal and intergroup relations, do not respond immediately and uniformly to media messages" (S. Chelcea, 2006, p. 89) or, according to P. Lazarsfeld, "most often, ideas migrate from the radio and newspapers to opinion leaders *and from* them reach the less active segments of the population" (S. Chelcea, 2006, p. 89).

An intermediate factor thus appears, the opinion leader, defined by exclusion by Gabriel Weimann as follows: "Opinion leaders are not leaders, in the common sense of the term and with its connotations. Opinion leaders are not authoritarian, charismatic leaders, but rather people who have the position of expert among those with the same social status as theirs and they are a source of advice on a certain issue or topic" (S. Chelcea, 2006, pp. 92–93).

* The diagram corresponding *to the two-step flow* model is as follows:

```
                    Sends                      Resends
        Source  ═══════════▶  Opinion leader  ═══════════▶  Their group
        of a message                           processed message to
```

(M. Coman, 1999, p. 117)

In conclusion, in the *two-step flow,* messages from the press messages do not directly reach individuals, but go through a complex system of mediation, while the content broadcast by the media does not have a monopoly on meanings; the meaning of a message is the result of a process of filtering and interpretation.

- The *cultivation* model launched by American sociologist Georg Gerbner is explained by W.J. Severin and J.W. Tankard in that prolonged exposure to the media leads to the establishment of "a vision of the common world, common roles and common values," (M. Coman, 1999, p. 119). The action of cultivation is manifested in two stages: a) the systematic reception of information, ideas, symbols, or values through the media; b) the formation of a representation of reality defined by the media.
- The *agenda* model is the result of research conducted by D.L. Shaw and M. McCombs and materialized in the study *The Emergence of Political Issues: The Agenda-Setting Function of the Press* published in 1977. Numerous subsequent studies confirmed the conclusions of the two authors, the basic idea being the following: "The press, intentionally or not, structures the topics of interest and the public debate. A working group always has an agenda, a list of topics, to be discussed in reverse order of importance. Normally, topics that are not on the agenda are not debated. The agenda model shows how the press and especially the news media ... have the power to focus the public's attention on a limited list of topics while ignoring others. As a result, some topics are insistently debated in the public space, and others are ignored" (Tim O'Sullivan in M. Coman, 1999, p. 121). Or, in other words: "The press may not be successful in telling people what to think, but it succeeds splendidly in telling people what to think about" (R. Farrar in M. Coman, 1999, p. 121–122). This situation leads to the conclusion that the priorities

of the press do not necessarily correspond to social priorities. Often, the media presents and imposes marginal aspects of social, political, economic life, etc. as major themes, essential aspects being left in the background. However, research has shown that the press exerts a slow influence on the public as well as that this influence affects, in particular, the representations of the masses about the world, hierarchies of any kind, in a word: the tools of environmental analysis.

We made this review of how the media can exert influence on individuals, starting from the concept of *public opinion* that Sonia Cristina Stan says is "the element of stability in a democratic system. It [the public opinion] ensures balance of the relationship between the Press and the Power. ... is the key to any act of manipulation through the press. Those who initiate the acts of manipulation aim to change it in their favor" (2004, p. 17).

To detect what exactly is an attempt to manipulate from whatever the media presents, the key term to be considered is *intent*. There is no such thing as unintentional manipulation, someone must intend to change someone's behavior, to make them act in their favor. "Demonstrating intentionality should often take the media out of the process of manipulation." If the intention does not exist, "but the reader is still misled, it is a *media error*, of which the press is guilty, but which is not manipulation" considers Sonia C. Stan in *Manipulation Through the Press* (2004, p. 33).

The same author proposes three contexts for the emergence of *media errors*:

1. publishing in good faith – when the press publishes false information that it believes to be true;
2. intuitions from the closing of the edition – unable to know the end of an event, the journalist anticipates;
3. fighting with the deadline – the continuous fight with the deadline decreases vigilance in verifying the information.

When it comes to deliberate misleading of the public, however, we are dealing with effective manipulation, which Stan classifies as follows: a) initiated by the press (for their interests); b) initiated by someone outside the press, but who uses the press to reach the target (the manipulated one). (S.C. Stan, 2004, p. 34).

a) The first category includes the manipulation that follows the interests of the journalist, the owner of the trust, and the distortions caused by the competitive nature of the profession.

Among the reasons that can cause the *journalist* to manipulate the truth in favor of their interests is the temptation of stardom, games or personal interests, small propaganda to accredit an idea that is favorable to their sources, working an angle, invention of subjects where there are none. As for the *owner,* it can act by disguised political interests and advertising restrictions – the embargo to disseminate disadvantageous information about those who buy time or advertising space with that media outlet.

*The existence of competition,*the desire to obtain an exclusive scoop and increase the rating result in the distortion of the truth to get a unique journalistic material.

b) "External manipulation is done without the consent of the press (but of course through it) in the name of major interests related to power, whether it is confined to the borders of a country or pursuing international interests. It is hard to find and hard to demonstrate ... Good psychologists, connoisseurs of human nature, usually work to put it into practice and it requires an elaborate apparatus for creating a positive image ... which would not impose itself and would not lead to favorable action. (whether it is called a vote, a favorable opinion, winning followers for various causes)" (S.C. Stan, 2004, pp. 35, 36, 37).

The three factors at the confluence of which a refined system of manipulation is born through the press are the *tendency of control by the powers that be, preserving the appearance of freedom of the press,* and *the commercial requirements* that influence any media and, inherently, its products. "From the union of the three results, the *reality presented by the press* and imposed as such, which is, most of the time, only a facet of reality" (S.C. Stan, 2004, p. 38).

Regarding *reality* and its *relationship to knowledge,* the field of sociology generated two divergent perspectives:

- *realistic*, according to which individuals have direct access to information from the environment, determining a direct correspondence between reality and knowledge;

- *constructivist*, which puts forward the hypothesis according to which reality may or may not be consciously constructed and which confers a privileged position to the journalist in his capacity as a *gatekeeper* in the process of selection and transmission of information.

Given the constructivist perspective, we will identify how the media can mislead its audience, as presented by S.C. Stan in *Manipulation through the Press* (2004, pp. 42–59).

Following the steps of a media production, in this case, a news story, several factors must be taken into account that can lead to the distortion of the initial information.

1. *international news agencies* – of the amount of news that a large agency receives, only a very small part is released. It would therefore be necessary to know the selection criteria and to have an insight into the interests that guide them;
2. *international financial groups* – support the interests of news agencies and follow the interests of the governments to which they belong, hiding the negative elements of the system;
3. *corporations, enterprises* – indirectly support various media institutions through advertising;
4. *editorial line* – influences the orientation of information;
5. the *journalist's characteristics* – values, prejudices, culture, etc.
6. *media criticism* – often, opinion pieces are published in daily newspapers, that present opinions which are contrary to those published in the rest of the newspaper, in an attempt to preserve the appearance of independence and plurality, increasing the credibility of the media.

The structuring of information in the press, the *form* in which it appears, and the *content of* articles are the main sectors in which the mechanism of manipulation can be developed and which we will analyze further.

Information structuring:

a) The *location and length of an article*. How information is organized and ranked in a newspaper influences the reader's perception of the importance of that information. Specialists in the press have all the necessary means to minimize the importance of information or, on the contrary, to highlight it. These means are:

- *The page where the article appears.* It has been psychologically proven that the information placed on the first and last page and the information printed on the first pages are read first. Those who choose this position consider them important. It also matters to place the article on an even or odd page (left or right, in journalistic jargon), as it is known that the information on the odd pages is harder to read.
- *Placement on-page.* The material at the top of the page (especially on the right), i.e, in *the optical center,* will be read first and is considered to support the entire page. An article placed next to *the binding of the newspaper* will be the hardest to read.
- *The length of an article.* The size of a news item on one page compared to the others or even the number of pages allocated to an event highlights the publication's priorities.
- *The section in which it appears.* Placing a news item that generally belongs in one section in another section plays a critical part in the interpretation that the reader will give it.

b) *The general framework in which the article is placed.* How an article is inserted next to others (which also have titles and photographs) influences its interpretation, the proximity of other materials sometimes generating unexpected effects: hilarious, ironic, or contrary to the original purpose.

c) *Photographs and other graphic materials.* Photos, drawings, diagrams, or graphics are eye-catching items. An inspiring image helps to express the article, having an immediate effect.

d) *The structure of the news: the inverted pyramid.* According to this typical scheme of organizing journalistic material, the most important thing is "why" – contextualization and interaction with other events. Often, the article is not read until the end, the context is thus overlooked. Besides, in case of lack of space, the last part of the material is the one that must be given up, which may make the event difficult to understand or contextualize.

The shape of information:

a) *Titles and subtitles.* The titles highlight an essential aspect that must emerge from reading the material. There is no room for explanations in the title, it only has the role of attracting attention, being the first to be read. Often, however, the title does not correspond to the actual

content of the article and even falsifies the facts that the material relates to, and an effect of manipulation emerges from this juxtaposition.
b) *Decontextualization.* The press tends to present the facts in isolation, as independent facts, unrelated to other aspects of reality, which are their causes or origins. When readers miss these elements, they cannot evaluate and analyze reality, making it much easier for the newspaper to impose its own opinion.

Decontextualization can be:

- *historical,* when the omission of the political, economic, cultural background no longer allows the analysis of the facts to understand the current situation;
- in the form of the *puzzle article,* characterized by the dispersion and fragmentation of different aspects and causes or consequences of the same fact in time and space. This type of material removes the perception of the event in its entirety.

c) *Written language.* The opinion of the journalist or the institution can be slipped into the information presented through several techniques:
- *Tone (biased language).* Using a pejorative, ironic, or triumphant tone can influence the perception of the event. And the use of quotation marks without the purpose of citation casts doubt or discredits.
- *Magic words.* Terms that have a positive (tolerance, development, flexibility, etc.) or negative connotation (illegal, radical, fundamentalist, etc.).
- *Associating words with deeds.* Some words are self-associated with certain people or groups. Thus, it is sufficient to mention the first term for it to evoke almost automatically the second (e.g.: "armed force" or "Basque radicalism").
- *Euphemisms and technicalities.* Words in these categories have the effect of reducing the value, of trivializing the real meaning of a word or phrase being modified (eg: "collateral victims" instead of "civilian deaths"). Technical language creates the impression of objectivity, and specialized language limits the readers' *access* to the text.
- *Biased expressions.* These are expressions that have entered the language of journalism that tend to induce certain ideas about the events reported ("law enforcement were forced to disperse the

protesters" – it is understood that the responsibility for the violence lies with the protesters).
- *Narrative style.* The styles in which topics are written – epic, satirical, lyrical, etc. – change the reader's perception.

d) *The language of images.* The photographs that accompany press texts are meant to *verify the* information in the text visually and make it credible, rendering it as realistic as possible. Often, however, images aim to influence the reception of information.
- *Photos that change the meaning of an article.* They distract the readers' attention through detail or may even contradict the text they illustrate.
- *Photos that look like tricks.* Certain elements that are accidentally captured around the foreground image can give a different meaning to the photograph.
- *Photo campaigns.* Images often seem to repeat themselves – even if they are never the same – because of the similar symbols they bear.

Information content:

a) *Selection of information sources.* Whether they are individuals, institutions, or documents, the sources have a decisive role in providing information. The opinion of witnesses to a particular event is often subjective, influenced by their views and personal values. Sources of any kind tend to follow their interests and impose their opinions, and the media sometimes omits the presentation of all the points of view of those involved.

b) *Fake news.* These news items or images were simply invented, difficult to detect and prove. Partially fake information is the most common practice in the press when it comes to intended manipulation. It consists in falsifying the information provided by any means.

c) *Rumors.* They appear in the form of news in which the author avoids giving precise information: the name of the personality, the place of the event, any element of identification, offering some landmarks, and operating with many allusions.

d) *Disguised advertising.* This involves inserting information in the news that promotes one's interests, without marking it as such or simply writing advertising material in a journalistic style. Masked advertising usually serves the interests of the owner, the media outlet, or even the journalist.

"The phenomenon of manipulation through the media is not easy to interpret. The Romanian press is also subject to the same gross acts of manipulation as the rest of the world, dictated by the economic or political interests of the media giants or governments. Even working to serve the public interest remains an ideal for the press in an ideal democracy, that self-regulatory mechanism of the press, professional ethics, will show journalists the path to take, without which the free press would disappear" (2004, p. 163).

CHAPTER IV: Politics and the Press

IV.1. Relationship Between Politicians and the Media

Claudiu Săftoiu wrote a textbook on *Political Journalism* in which the relationship of interdependence between the press and politicians was analyzed, as well as how the transmission of information between the two parties is accomplished. According to Săftoiu, "political journalism represents that segment of mass communication that achieves – in a continuous process of mutual dependence – the link between media consumers and the political message, at directly connected national and transnational levels. Political journalism has a decisive influence on the power of penetration, the quality and coherence of the political message" (2003, p. 7).

Săftoiu emphasizes that "the relationship between the press and the political environment is a force field, in which opponents seek to achieve their specific goals. Tensions between competitors range from fair negotiations and exchanges of information to overt intimidation and mutual obstruction. "Moreover, the mass media have become essential for politicians, who turned them into tools used to persuade the target audience, the last 20 years have led to the creation of a new form of distribution of the political message: political communication. For this form of expression of ideas to be put into practice, several media products adapted to the new "requirements were built" (C. Săftoiu, 2003, p. 12).

The foundation of any press material, however, is set by the journalist who represents the link between the politician and the public. Therefore, it is considered that "if the political message was received poorly by the electorate, interventions or opacifications may have appeared in the process of receiving and communicating it forward, sometimes from political journalists," as the situation is often invoked where members of the press "document, collect, analyze and write a news item based on several influencing factors that affect their work" (C. Săftoiu, 2003, pp. 13–14).

"Newsworthy materials are dramatic, conflictual, and violent. The media is forced to create news capable of attracting mass attention. Presenting a news story in drama mode is one of the tricks of working in the media. A dramatic situation begins with an exciting action, followed by an event that breaks routine. The conflict escalates into an action that reaches a climax ... and the end is represented by an unexpected exit from the respective situation ... This format gives the information coherence and creates a story that is easy to follow and understand .... / Consequently, conflict sells the news. The media often tends to highlight the conflict. Even where it is not desirable. ... the press seeks to sharpen conflicts, *to stoke the fire*, because the public is taught to react and get emotionally involved in conflict situations" (C. Săftoiu, 2003, p. 24–25).

In journalistic terms, conflict often translates into *a press scandal* which "is considered the recent event that arouses attention and general interest, involves personalities from the public, political or business world and generates violent reactions, with important consequences in terms of the protagonists' image [the problem *of the image crisis* will be treated in detail in the next subchapter]. The press scandal occurs when the daily press consumer is injected with a constant dose of *typographic adrenaline* in the pages of the newspaper: threatening headlines, warning reports, flashy photos. The preference for the superlative, exception, exclusive and morbid leads to the habit of peppery tastes that burn the palate. A reader thus trained ... receives with ease any information interpreted or presented in an excessive regime" (C. Săftoiu, 2003, p. 29).

Because of the struggle for audiences and implicitly for profit, political journalism has not been deprived of conflicting approaches. "Borrowing elements of sports and military jargon, the press has populated political life with a series of fictitious representations of good and evil, as in a daily re-editing of the biblical text. The moralistic commentary contained in journalistic terms referring to the political world led to the creation of genre-specific expressions and phrases: political personalities became *characters*; parties – *gangs*; political actions became *battles and wars*; strategies – *dirty games* [gradually, this language has been adopted by certain political communicators who often use it in situations of conflict, to characterize their opponents]. Nicknames, ironic, contemptuous or defamatory appellations of the political personalities of the moment are common things in the Romanian political journalism" (C. Săftoiu, 2003, p. 30).

In the 1990s, the theory of *media intrusion into politics* was enunciated, which calls into question, first of all, the intervention of television in political communication. "The reality offered by the new journalistic environment proves increasingly weak links with the real existence of the activity, rhythm, and sense of politics. Distorted by the preference for the spectacular, which reduces almost everything to rumor or gossip, the importance of the institution of the political party gradually but constantly disappeared." News centered on inefficiency or personal failures has led to widespread public skepticism about the capabilities of current political individuals and institutions. "This relentless trend has created the phenomenon of *video malaise* (in French) – a visual distaste for politics. The appetite for showiness in the media deteriorates the way political life is reflected, by presenting a negative load of political bodies or organizations meant to ensure social balance. ... Moreover, under the influence of the western commercial society, politics has become a consumer good. The doctrines have lost their importance ... while the political victory is now obtained by capitalizing on the individual charisma" (C. Săftoiu, 200 3, pp. 31, 38).

Against the background of these changes in approach, the media people are the ones who offer to the public: 1) hierarchical and value structures; 2) emphasis on the importance of certain events or persons, depending on the amount of information presented at a given time; 3) daily priorities (attracting or distracting attention from political debates).

"The values of those who have control over the newspapers (media outlet owners) are completely different from those of journalists. Although they claim to respect the truth, honesty, and virtue, they seek, above all, to make a profit and to make propaganda, for a specific purpose" (C. Săftoiu, 2003, p. 33). Along with this characteristic of the domestic media, Săftoiu notes "the moralizing tendency contained in the political interest messages and transmitted by the general attitude of the newspapers towards the social and political actuality avoids the application of a unified evaluation standard. Therefore, the imminent tabloidization of the entire Romanian press – in the short and long term – determines the approach of reality in an exclusively subjective regime" (C. Săftoiu, 2003, p. 40).

Regardless of how the information is presented, the press also fulfills certain functions *within* the political system, that can be deduced from the above considerations:

- Presenting the audience with information;
- Interpretation of news and facts;

- Influencing public opinion;
- Ensuring interactivity between politics and the public.

These functions are joined by those that the media exercises concerning the politician (C. Săftoiu, 2003, pp. 43, 44, 45):

a) *Supervision* – "the media manipulates the interest and attention of the public through investigations and sensational revelations while supervising the event priorities. ... Negative publicity produces disastrous effects on a political approach, and the effort to rectify the consequences of such negative publicity is doubled."
b) *Social legitimation* – "public recognition of the politician is their very reason for being. In this sense, the political environment must obey the norms of collaboration with the media."
c) *Interpretation* – "the interpretive methods of the media form and distort the opinion on political phenomena, directing their impact on the life of individuals. ... Marked forms of control and manipulation by the media are represented by the following actions:
   - removing a message, event, or political phenomenon from context;
   - reducing the space for presenting a message, event, or political phenomenon;
   - editorial limitations;
   - personal or ideological perspective.
d) *Information filter.*

As we saw in the title of this subchapter, it is not only the media that can influence the politician but also the politicians manifest their control over the press. Given the fact that this reality is not the subject of the present study, we will limit ourselves to establishing the context in which this influence takes place and to the presentation of the most common forms of manipulation coming from politicians.

"Manipulation in journalism presupposes the existence of well-defined journalistic rules. The possibility to influence the information is directly related to the understanding of journalistic rules and norms; as a consequence, many successful public relations advisers are former media professionals. The information provided by the media is vulnerable, precisely because reporters have deadlines and obstacles to overcome. They base their work on information from various sources also because they are required to be quick and present dramatic facts" (C. Săftoiu, 2003, p. 52).

Against the background of the inherent vulnerabilities that characterize the manufacturing process of media products, some of the most common forms of influence appear (C. Săftoiu, 2003, pp. 53–63):

- *manipulation of deadlines* – information provided by an important political figure about an equally important fact just before the deadline for submission can be easily taken over and subsequently related in a non-critical manner; politicians issue a press release shortly before the closing of editions, relying on the fact that journalists will no longer be able to verify the information disseminated through the press release and will report the data without requesting the reaction of the incriminated persons;
- *manipulating breaking news moments and high rating moments* – to obtain a maximum audience, politicians take advantage of the increased rating of certain formats to communicate exclusive information in *prime time*;
- *manipulation of the obligation to cite the sources* – when a credible source refuses to confirm certain information or when it *is missing* at that very moment, the press loses the element of confirmation and can no longer edit/disseminate the material;
- *manipulation through predictable events* – due to the lists of events that reach the newsrooms daily through news agencies, politicians secure free coverage of their actions;
- *manipulating the media's access to political events / exclusive interviews* – through such a strategy, reporters are denied/conditioned access to the venue or a certain personality;
- *manipulation through pre-packaged news or feature articles* – political advisers exploit the reporters' lack of time and provide them with ready-made articles that provide an advantage to the point of view of the politician or the institution they represent.

IV.2. Media Crisis and the Social Image

The case study presented in this paper provides an analysis of how the press publicized the disclosures of the Securitate files, in the case of Mona Muscă. Given the fact that we considered that this situation meets the necessary criteria, we included it in the category of *media crises* and we underlined those details applicable to the analyzed case.

According to Ion Chiciudean, "*the media crisis* is a particular case of the communication crisis determined by the media intervention in the evolution of this crisis, an intervention dictated by the lack of official, coherent and timely information on the usual communication channels. Compensating for the information deficit is constantly requested by the public, which thus offers the media the opportunity to fill the existing information vacuum and turn into an authorized information provider, interpreter, evaluator and privileged sender" (1999, p. 69).

The author considers that these crises occur unexpectedly and are strongly emotional, while their intensity depends on the social importance of the event that gave rise to them, the social consequences they generate, and the degree of public involvement. Media crises of great interest to the press usually give rise to unpleasant news for the organization/person involved. Because, as a rule, there are few witnesses to the event, the public opinion is formed by what is seen, heard, or read in the press. In most cases, the media crisis is extinguished or loses traction long before the effects of the event that produced it disappear (I. Chiciudean, 1999, p. 71).

"In its acute form, the media crisis causes the loss of control of information and the public. If the response to the crisis is not as expected if the first information that the organization [person] provides is not credible or there were cases or attempts to mislead the public in the past of the organization, the public will turn to another credible source which quickly provides what they want: information about the event" (I. Chiciudean, 1999, p. 71). As a consequence, the public will obtain the desired data from other sources that will build a new image of the person/event per their own perceptions and interests. At the same time, the media crisis causes increased visibility of the protagonists, which can lead to the discovery of other already existing problems. The consequences of these steps can affect the public's perception for a long time, requiring great efforts to regain credibility.

"The media loves crises because they produce victims and culprits. Both categories are sources of news that must be exploited and transmitted quickly to the public. ... In most cases, the pressure of the media leads to the acceleration of investigations, out of the desire to announce who is guilty and why. The pressure will be even greater as the scandal seems to be rising (involving politicians, businesses or public institutions) and directly related to the perception that they try to hide or cover up the facts behind *so-called* confidential or secret information" (I. Chiciudean, 1999, pp. 73, 74). The same author presents the hypothesis launched by Clarence Jones in his book *Winning with the News Media,* according to which the media have already developed a set of criteria, a grid of morality for evaluating and classifying the good and the bad. According to this, reporters tend to identify with the victims of society [after they decide, in advance, which side they are on] and to use them as main sources (I. Chiciudean, 1999, p. 73).

During the media crisis, the roles of the media in providing and evaluating information are privileged, the press is the main communication channel to which the public appeals. Thus, members of the press transmit both pure information and their own opinions, in the form of editorials and comments, having a decisive role in the process of shaping public opinion. In the spirit of journalistic practices, the person or institution in the spotlight will receive all kinds of labeling according to each stage of the crisis. Because of this, the media crisis often causes an *image crisis*.

Roger Muchielli, quoted by Chiciudean, defines the image as "the representation or idea that individuals create in their minds, regarding an environment or a segment of the public as a result of receiving information about a social object" (1999, p. 11). "The image is considered part of the social representation, its stable element (core) corresponds to the value system in line with the given culture and social norms. The importance of the image is given by its possibility to contribute to the shaping of behaviors and the orientation of social communications in various ways of dissemination, propagation, propaganda" (I. Chiciudean, 1999, p. 11).

"General psychology approaches image in close connection with the components of the attitudinal-volitional act: perception – evaluation – opinion – attitude – conviction. The stages covered from the reception of the social object to the shaping of the image are conditioned by knowledge, value appreciation, confrontation of arguments, initial value verdict (opinion), stable value verdict (conviction), etc. The image, according to this concept, is the result of the evaluation processes initiated in the psychological structures of the individual, aimed at obtaining opinions and, later, convictions. As a result, the influence of the individual cannot be achieved through a transfer of opinions or beliefs, but only through their stimulation, triggering and generation in the individual's mind with the help of the argument" (Neculai Bălan in I. Chiciudean, 1999, p. 11).

"Social images correspond to the set of values in line with culture, tradition, the system of collective beliefs, given social norms and they contribute to the shaping of behaviors and orientation of social communications. Social images are elaborated through and in relation with social communication and, therefore, it is believed that the dynamics of communication and the dynamics of social images intersect with the elements of the collective mind, of which mentalities and the interpretation given by people and social groups play fundamental roles" (I. Chiciudean, 1999, p. 14).

"Any communication is made in a certain informational and interpretive range. ... All areas of human activity with their own symbols and language are construed in such ranges in which information is specifically processed. ... Within each social information range of interpretation there are changes, including discontinuities (radical changes). Each horizon of interpretation contains (maintains) erroneous or simplistic ways of processing, in addition to the correct ways of interpreting social information. The crises that appear in the economic, political, ideological field prove this.

Distortions and errors that occur in the way information is processed within the range of interpretation are the main causes of image distortions, causing, in some situations, even image distortions. This is possible because social images are a result of the way information is received and processed in the social spaces in which images are construed. In these spaces, the shaping of images involves uncontrollable elements (values, cultural models, traditions, customs, mentalities, beliefs, etc.), but also controllable elements (interests, decisions of some centers of power, etc.), which give a certain orientation to the processes of shaping social images. "The problems are much more acute in the situation when certain ranges of interpretation serve as means of legitimizing the social image aggression of people, organizations, and nations that are situated in other ranges of interpretation" (I. Chiciudean, 1999, p. 15).

In Chiciudean's opinion, "the *image* is the public reflection of the reputation, personality or identity of an organization. ... A coherent, positive image gives stability and success in the competition for resources and audiences. Also, it is less vulnerable to attacks by competition and less exposed to the risks of facing a crisis. On the contrary, the reduction of compatibility between what the world does, says, and believes about the organization, as well as the change of the polarity of the image towards the negative direction of public evaluations, determines the decrease of the organization's performance, the reduction of market share and even its crisis" (1999, p. 79).

As far as politicians are concerned, the pressure of public opinion can determine the preoccupation of decision-making centers to give immediate answers to the issues raised by public opinion, which represent only types of processing and interpretation of some situations and not the reality. In this case, one of the consequences that appear is that politics will tend to make *an image game* because politics will always be forced to have an image strategy. It is a rule of the game, and a successful policy cannot be conceived outside this binding image strategy. When concerns are centered on the image, to the detriment of reality itself, failure becomes only a matter of time (P. Dobrescu, A. Bârgăoanu, 2003, p. 30).

Chiciudean defines the image crisis as "that deterioration of notoriety, reputation and public trust to such an extent that it endangers the functioning or existence of an organization" (1999, p. 80). We consider that these opinions are also valid in the case of a person/personality.

One of the main causes that determine the appearance of an image crisis is the fluctuations of credibility that cause mistrust. The media plays a decisive role in this process when it filters and transmits messages to the public that confirm or refute the verticality of someone's character.

In Ion Chiciudean's opinion, the image crisis is characterized by the following features:

a) *It does not appear suddenly.* Unlike media crises, the image crisis has a slower and more complex evolution. Its development is influenced by the number of categories of public involved in the process, by the communication capacity of the organization, and by the hostility of the communication environment. Changes in the beliefs of individuals are slower than those of opinions or attitudes, while evaluation, which results in an image being built, is influenced by the deep beliefs of individuals.
b) *It overlaps and is determined by an identity crisis specific to the organizational culture.* It can, in turn, lead to an identity crisis.
c) According to Hary Levinson quoted by Chiciudean, an exhaustive analysis of the identity of an organization or person involves the following elements: what it does; what it says; what people think it should be (1999, p. 83).

d) It is *more difficult to identify an image crisis than other types of crises*. It requires more complex analyses and evaluations, led by specialized structures that identify the attitudes and trust of employees and the external public.
e) *The effects of the image crisis are manifest in the long run.* The credibility of an organization/person is difficult to obtain, it is maintained with great efforts, and it is regained with even greater difficulty, and at very high costs. The effects of the crisis cease once it is resolved through restructuring, redefining goals and objectives, eliminating the causes of incidents, accidents, and conflicts. The image crisis is cumulative and profound. Because of it, the organization can remain stigmatized throughout its existence, if nothing is done to restore the public image (1999, p. 86).

Among the most important effects of an image crisis are the following: a possible loss of credibility and legitimacy, blocking the development process in the entire field of activity or the entire branch but it can also cause a change in the strategic mission of the organization as seen by the public (1999, pp. 87–88).

CHAPTER V: Case Study

V.1. Media Approach to the Topic of Mona Muscă

In this part of the paper, we will make an applied analysis of how the concepts of *information and manipulation* were illustrated in the Romanian press when the Securitate files were revealed. To reflect the attitude of the media, we chose the case of *Mona Muscă,* a controversial topic that was widely debated by most dailies at the time.

As it appears from the theoretical chapters presented above, the media can choose, process, and transmit to the public those aspects of reality that they consider significant. Journalists have the power to choose from the informative mix those events that they decide to highlight. After the data is passed through the member of the press's own grid of values, and the editorial body decides that they are in line with the editorial policy of the publication or radio or television station, the information takes the form of messages, of journalistic materials.

Depending on what importance is given to it, the news item can be placed in the last pages, therefore being easily overlooked by readers, or can occupy the central part of the first page, with the title of exclusivity and with a potential to spark a real media crisis. The first and most important destination of these materials is the public, that heterogeneous mass of individuals who sometimes have nothing in common other than the fact that they receive the same media material, but who need the media to be able to navigate the contemporary society.

One of the most important roles played by the press is *agenda setting*: the role of setting priorities on the individual's agenda. Journalists draw up an imaginary list of topics of primary interest that are to be dispatched to the public to be debated and around which different currents of opinion are formed. Along with instrumental information, the media also disseminates a range of views on events that do not directly affect the public, but only their perceptions or opinions about certain people or topics of general interest. Political life is one of these, a topic of discussion often encountered, but which is a priority only for a small number of individuals. Usually, the opinions of those who receive media messages on political issues are heard only on the occasion of events such as elections or referenda. However, there are other tools for testing public opinion, opinion polls being the most common.

However, the media have become the main opinion shaper in recent decades, being the main means by which political communicators convey their messages. As we have seen before, both politicians and journalists or media outlet owners can impact the form and content of these messages in different ways. The most common changes lead to disinformation or even manipulation of the public. The methods used in these cases differ from one subject to another and the context in which they appear and are presented.

What is certain is that, following the receipt of distorted information and subjected to a different process than that of objective information, the audience may form wrong perceptions, thus manifesting their support or disapproval in certain situations. Moreover, when the article has the power to trigger a media crisis, the protagonists can be strongly and sometimes even irrevocably affected.

The object of the present study is the analysis of how the media presented the information when the Securitate files were exposed. To illustrate the extent to which the reports were made objectively, or manipulated public opinion, we chose to analyze one of the most controversial cases, that of Mona Muscă (Appendix 1).

V.2 Development of Events in the Case of Mona Muscă

Lavinia Şandru, an MP from the National Initiative Party (PIN), declared on August 8, 2006, on Realitatea TV, that the liberal Mona Muscă had a *file of collaborator of the former Securitate*. According to the quoted source, this file had already reached the National College for the Study of Securitate Archives (CNSAS), being part of the group of 29 declassified files, on which SRI had put the national security stamp.

On August 10, MP Mona Muscă presented her two Securitate files to the press. One was a surveillance file, under which she was watched by the former secret police, and the second was a network collaborator file. Monica Nicoară (her name from the first marriage) signed a commitment to the Securitate and received a conspiratorial name, *Dana*. Although she collaborated with the Securitate, Mona Muscă initially said that she only provided verbal notes to the Vice-Dean of the University of Timişoara, where she worked as an assistant.

During the CNSAS hearing on August 22, Mona Muscă acknowledged that her relationship with the Securitate was not limited to 15 pieces of information about foreign students. During the few hours of discussions with the members of the CNSAS College, Mona Muscă was put face to face with new informative notes, signed by *Dana,* about two of her colleagues from the Philology Department in Timişoara. Asked if there were other documents, Muscă said she did not remember exactly. This was the first moment when Mona Muscă said that she was wrong and that she regretted her collaboration with the Securitate. She motivated her gesture by saying that it was about the *safety of foreign students and the safety of Romania.* As a result, she published her file on the Internet. On August 14, 2006, the Central Permanent Bureau of the National Liberal Party (PNL) decided to propose to the Permanent Delegation the exclusion of deputy Mona Muscă from the party for signing a commitment to collaborate with the Securitate.

Five days later, the PNL Bucharest leadership decided to ask deputy Mona Muscă to resign from Parliament before receiving the final verdict from CNSAS.

PIN MP Lavinia Şandru, who announced, for the first time, that Mona Muscă was a collaborator of the Securitate, declared on September 17 that the two positive notes that Mona Muscă gave to the Securitate under the conspiratorial name *Dana* were used as recommendations for recruiting future collaborators. The information was confirmed by CNSAS members.

The college decided on September 19 that Mona Muscă cooperated with the secret police. On the same day, the deputy announced that she would challenge the decision of the College in court. The trial took place on October 12, 2006.

On March 7, the Bucharest Court of Appeals rejected the appeal made by Mona Muscă and ruled that the verdict given by CNSAS remained valid: Mona Muscă was a collaborator of the secret police under the conspiratorial name of *Dana.* On the same day, the MP announced her retirement from politics and her intention to appeal to the European Court of Human Rights in Strasbourg.

A CURS survey, conducted between September 18 and October 2, 2006, on a sample of 1,053 people, with a margin of error of three percent, showed that 50 percent of the subjects still had a good and very good opinion about Mona Muscă. This had decreased by nine percent in the measurements made by CURS, the last survey, in July, crediting her with 59 percent in terms of good and very good opinion.

On November 19, Mona Muscă reached the lowest confidence level in 2006. If in January the former PNL leader capitalized almost 60 % of Romanians' options, in November, according to an Insomar poll, only 29 % of those surveyed gave her their trust.

In 2006, Mona Muscă was named the *Most Appreciated Politician* within project *10 for Romania,* carried out by Realitatea TV. In 2007, Muscă took fifth place in the same section.

V.3. Analysis Material

To observe the direction followed by the journalistic approach in the presentation of the events in the case of Mona Muscă, we chose the written press, respectively two dailies in direct competition, which have close editions and address mainly the same target audience, but which approaches everyday events differently from an editorial point of view.

The publications followed are *Cotidianul* and *Gândul.* Both are generalist dailies, which privilege information but present it differently. Founded in 1991 by Ion Rațiu, *Cotidianul* was taken over and relaunched in 2004 by *Academia Cațavencu.* Currently, the editorial director is the journalist Robert Turcescu. *Gândul* was founded in 2005 by the resigning editorial team from the newspaper *Adevărul* and led by Cristian Tudor Popescu.

Both dailies had an intermediate format, between A2 and A3, and were constantly concerned with improving the image and quality, the aim of this approach being to gain as many target audiences as possible. Besides, interactivity is privileged in both publications, the online version.

According to Cristian Tudor Popescu quoted by *Gândul,* the newspaper is aimed at readers aged 45 on average, with higher education and an appreciable, middle-class income. *Cotidianul* targets people with decision-making roles such as managers or people in the administration, but also those who work in the liberal professions, such as doctors or teachers. In the 32 pages of the publication (16 during the publication of the articles in the case of Mona Muscă) only photos and advertisements were in full color, the text being printed in black to preserve the note of sobriety.

According to the Romanian Circulation Audit Bureau (BRAT), the *Gândul* newspaper sold 4,404,276 copies between July and December 2006, out of a gross circulation of 6,145,950, with an average of 950,000 copies per month. In terms of audience, it is an average of 164,000 readers per edition, according to the latest data from the National Audience Survey, corresponding to the measurement period July 25, 2005 – July 16, 2006.

Cotidianul addresses a premium, elite, high-income target audience with higher education according to Dragos Stanca, general publishing director of the Realitatea-Catavencu Group quoted in the newspaper's pages. This daily newspaper's forum section is one of the most accessed, with sometimes dozens of users commenting on the events of the day. Also, several sections are dedicated to interactivity with readers in both versions of the newspaper – print and online.

Thanks to book collections and, more recently, encyclopedias published with the publication, the daily's audience has grown. The average circulation was about 350,000 copies per month between July and December 2006. The number of copies sold on Wednesdays, together with the novels from the Literature collection, reached 50,000 (data to be confirmed by BRAT which audits the publication starting from this year).

We chose these two newspapers based on the criterion of the target audience that corresponded to the type of audience targeted by Mona Muscă in her political approaches and speeches. We also took into account the rather large circulation compared to other publications that prioritize information, as well as the fact that the editorial teams of the two newspapers include opinion leaders such as Cristian Tudor Popescu, Bogdan Chireac, Robert Turcescu, Corina Dragotescu, Traian Ungureanu, and so on.

Consequently, we followed the idea that the public tends to pay special attention to messages that are transmitted by people considered to be formal or informal opinion shapers, all the more so as the target audience meets the criteria necessary to pass the message on, fulfilling the role of opinion leader in the communities in which they operate.

V.4. Methods of Analysis

Conceptual or quantitative content analysis and *empirical interpretation of qualitative data* are the two main methods we approached to obtain the necessary data on which the conclusions of the study will be based.

According to Mircea Agabrian, "content analysis is a technique for collecting and organizing information in a format that allows researchers to make inferences about the characteristics and meaning of messages (written and oral) and social communication artifacts" (2006, p. 17), or in short, a message decoding system.

The "method" operates from the perspective that verbal behavior is a form of human behavior, the flow of symbols is part of the flow of events, and the process of communication is an aspect of the historical process. ... Content analysis is a technique that aims to describe what is said about a given subject, with optimal objectivity, precision, and generality, in a given place at a given time (Lasswell et al., 1952, p. 34).

"With the help of content analysis, researchers have the opportunity to compare the content of many texts, which they can analyze using quantitative (graphs, tables) and qualitative techniques (semantic networks, matrices)" (Mircea Agabrian, 2006, p. 18). This research technique also called non-reactive – those studied are not aware that they are part of such a project – uses secondary sources and data. "It is important to examine secondary sources, because the nature of such information may indicate intentional or unintentional inclinations that may alter their understanding. Using content analysis, the researcher examines the content of documents produced by social institutions, typically the media, to highlight the specifics of social phenomena" (Mircea Agabrian, 2006, p. 19).

Researchers use content analysis to study, among other things:

- trends in the topics approached by news newspapers;
- the ideological tone of the editorialists;
- the answers to the open-ended questions in the questionnaires
- ideological themes in the speeches of political leaders, etc.

E. Woodrum quoted by M. Agabrian notes: "Content analysis remains a research method with great potential for the study of beliefs, organizations, attitudes and human relationships" (2006, p. 20).

The objective of any such quantitative analysis "is to count the key categories and measure the quantities distributed by variables. In this way, it is compatible with the nomothetic approach, i.e. it aims to produce generalizable conclusions" (M. Agabrian, 2006, p. 24).

"Beyond the diversity of content analysis, the approach focuses on the content analysis of the text" (M. Agabrian, 2006, p. 26). In this case, "the researcher uses objective and systematic counting and recording procedures, but also subjective interpretation procedures, thus making a quantitative and qualitative description of the symbolic content of the text" (M.Agabrian, 2006, p. 29).

According to Septimiu Chelcea, the following steps are followed in the quantitative content analysis (2004, pp. 263–281):

1. The choice of the research topic – its presentation will focus on a concise description of the nature of the problem to be investigated;
2. Establishing materials for analysis
3. Sampling – it is necessary when the number of documents is too large to be analyzed as a whole, so it is divided into three categories:
   a) selection of sources – from the multitude of information sources that surround us, we choose the one that best suits the analysis we are following and which is in line with the considered
   b) sampling of documents – for the analysis of the written press, we can do this guided by the prestige of the newspapers and by the criterion of representativeness;
   c) sampling from documents – we can choose different types of articles, from editorial to report, depending on the author or topic (if we initially opted for the written press).
4. Analysis procedures:
   a) *frequency analysis* – word frequency counting and making lists of typical words are standard techniques in content analysis, and according to Agabrian, "word frequency sets usually indicate important topics in the text. ... The analyst encodes the frequency of the recording units determining how many times each word or theme appears in the text" (2006, p. 76);
   b) *trend analysis* – is used to highlight the attitude of the issuer concerning a certain idea/person/event; in fact, analysts code the intensity of the attitude (the force of a message in a certain direction);

c) *evaluative analysis* – deals with the study of attitude;
d) *contingency analysis* – highlights the association structure of terms or concepts in the text; the analysis refers to the manifested or latent intention of the sender to use certain keywords.
e) *definition of recording units* – involves establishing the element that will be used to measure *variables* ("a definable and measurable concept, idea or construct that varies, i.e. has different values for different cases or units. ... At the beginning of the measurement process, the researcher conceptualizes and operationalizes each variable. Conceptualization is the process by which a construct/concept is refined using a conceptual or theoretical definition;" M. Agabrian, 2006, pp. 47–48); the process of content analysis starts from a variable and continues with the development of a measure for its empirical observation;
f) *coding* – represents the transformation of observations into categories and classifications, assigning a number or a symbol to each information item or parts of a sentence, for subsequent quantitative analysis. The process of organizing into categories is a defining feature of textual content analysis.
5. Implementation of techniques or interpretation of data
6. Fidelity of content analysis coding – fidelity is ensured when, after repeated measurements of the same material, similar conclusions result. To achieve the highest levels of fidelity, the boundaries of the categories with maximum details must be defined
7. Validity – "refers to the matching of categories with conclusions, as well as to the ability to generalize the results at the theoretical level" (M.Agabrian, 2006, p. 123).

Several researchers, including Berelson, Krippendorff, and Weber, have concluded that this method of research is a systematic, replicable technique by which the numerous words of a message are compressed into fewer content categories based on clear coding rules. "Equally, the simplification and categorization of written materials, their structuring to be introduced in dedicated programs (*software*) are part of the content analysis" (M. Agabrian, 2006, p. 22).

V.5. Information and Manipulation in the Case of Mona Muscă: Content Analysis

We chose this topic of study due to the increased interest of the media for the subject of uncovering the Securitate files and especially for the information related to Mona Muscă. At the time, she was one of the highest-ranking politicians and one of the initiators of several laws condemning those with ties to the communist system. Also, Mona Muscă had repeatedly expressed her disapproval of the communist regime and the Securitate.

Following the media coverage of the chain of events, starting with the information according to which Mona Muscă was a collaborator of the Securitate until her withdrawal from political life following the confirmation of the verdict of collaborator with the secret police given by CNSAS, Mona Muscă's credibility decreased significantly. Opinion polls showed that her social image was negatively affected in this case and that public confidence in the former MP had fallen from 60 percent in January to 29 percent in November 2006.

Given that the media were the main and often the only source of information for the general public, we started from the following question: *To what extent did newspapers report objectively or, on the contrary, manipulated the public opinion, influencing public perception?*

The objective is to explore and understand the texts that make up the chosen sample, to reveal the conclusions that demonstrate what type of message was issued by the selected dailies: information or manipulation.

The data was collected from the print media. This option is because the publications had the opportunity to present and comment more broadly on the subject, as opposed to the audiovisual where time constraints limited the allocated space. Besides, dailies, thanks to the editorial structure, provide daily space in columns or even whole pages, in some cases, for opinion materials.

We chose two of the daily publications that dealt primarily with the Mona Muscă case both in the main moment of the crisis, between August and September, and later.

The newspapers in question, *Cotidianul* and *Gândul*, which we discussed in detail in sub-chapter IV.4.2, are aimed at a large premium audience that identifies with the audience Mona Muscă addressed herself during her political career. As a result, this public may change the data in opinion polls in the event of media manipulation.

Starting from this conclusion, we studied the online issues of the two dailies for a period of 9 months, between August 9, 2006 – May 9, 2007, and we selected the relevant articles for this study. Before this approach, we checked, for a week, to what extent the content of the digital version coincided with the prints of the respective publications and we concluded that the articles were identical. we chose the ones focused on the Mona Muscă case in the series of revelations about the Securitate files: news, reports, editorials, comments but also other materials in which the character was mentioned in the respective context. The selection was made according to the appearance of the name *Mona Muscă* both in the headlines and inside the articles.

This approach resulted in a representative sample of 153 articles (80 from *Cotidianul* and 73 from *Gândul*), of different sizes (500–6000 ≥ characters), which cover most journalistic genres (from news taken from the *Mediafax* agency and published in *Gândul,* up to notes or tickets), are located on various pages and in various sections and are written by different authors or news agencies.

To classify and analyze the articles, we considered that the most appropriate *registration unit* in the present situation is the entire document, namely, the *article*.

The next step was to establish seven main categories (*variables)* in which the 153 texts fell, depending on the angle and the message transmitted. This method aimed at analyzing the frequency of topics in the selected articles (Table 4 *Appendix 1)* and the relevant results will be presented below.

In this approach, we also considered a series of keywords (analyzed in detail in the following pages) which were the basis for the introduction of categories in the texts. Among the studied words are the verbs used for attributing statements: *he said, explained, claimed, tried,* nouns such as *victim, mistake, morality,* etc., but also relevant proper names in the analysis: *Dana* and *Eva*. we also took into account the tone of the article, as well as the grounds on which the statements were based.

The names of the categories were chosen empirically, taking into account the topics addressed in the journalistic discourse, and this allocation was made after studying the analyzed material:

1. Objective presentation of information
2. Condemnation/accusation of the character
3. Condemning the deeds of the Securitate (in general)
4. Support for the character
5. The character mentioned in passing, without influencing the article
6. Launching of hypotheses
7. Other

The *Other* category contains those articles that do not fall into any of the above categories of topics and that, due to the very small number, are not relevant as a separate group.

Topics represented by categories were coded with numbers from 1 to 7, to facilitate the analysis process (Table 1, *Appendix 1*). The texts were marked with one of these numbers to be classified.

Of the total texts, 57 (37.2 %) were included in the category *Condemnation/accusation of the character* (34 in *Cotidianul* and 23 in *Gândul*), while 41 (26.7 %) were aimed at the *objective presentation of information* (15 in *Cotidianul* and 26 in *Gândul*). *The mention of the character in passing, without influencing the article* (12 in *Cotidianul* and 12 in *Gândul*) was found in 24 articles (15.6 %) while 11 materials out of a total of 153, i.e. 7.1 %, were aimed at *supporting the character.* (9 in *Cotidianul* and 2 in *Gândul*). It should be mentioned that in the articles belonging to the last category no praiseworthy or praiseworthy words/expressions were used towards the character. We chose to include it in this section since the data was presented in favor of the character or in her defense.

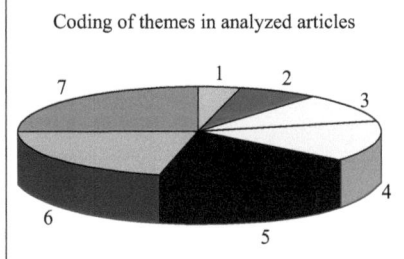

Following this method of analysis, what emerged is that the journalistic discourse of both dailies was based on the condemnation of the character Mona Muscă, objectivity not being the main feature of the analyzed articles. There is a difference of 11 articles in favor of *Cotidianul*, which published the most accusatory materials and the fewest objective ones – 15 – compared to 26 published in *Gândul*. Both dailies published 12 articles each whose main topics were not focused on the case of Mona Muscă and which mentioned her name only in passing, without secondary implications in the text message. However, the Muscă example was given whenever there was a suitable context. Regarding the *support of the character*, *Gândul* adopted a radical editorial policy, with only two pro-Mona Muscă articles, while in the pages of *Cotidianul* we found 9 positive materials. This first analysis revealed the tendency of the *Cotidianul* newspaper to present the information subjectively, imposing its own opinions through the journalistic discourse.

After analyzing the frequency of topics in articles, we were able to calculate the attitudinal coefficient, TA. First, we subtracted, according to the formula, the number of unfavorable units from the total of favorable units. The figure obtained was divided by the total number of units and by the total number of items, respectively. The partial attitudinal coefficients were negative, -0.31 for *Cotidianul* and -0.28 for *Gândul*. The total attitudinal coefficient, -0.3, revealed the increased tendency to criticize the character and to use a negative discourse towards her, which is obvious in the case of both dailies.

The study further involved the analysis of the frequency of journalistic genres in the selected articles (Table 2, Appendix 1). We considered this classification relevant to observe to what extent the materials centered on the subject of Mona Muscă were treated from the point of view of opinion or information. It is well known that the editorial policy of each publication is reflected primarily in editorials.

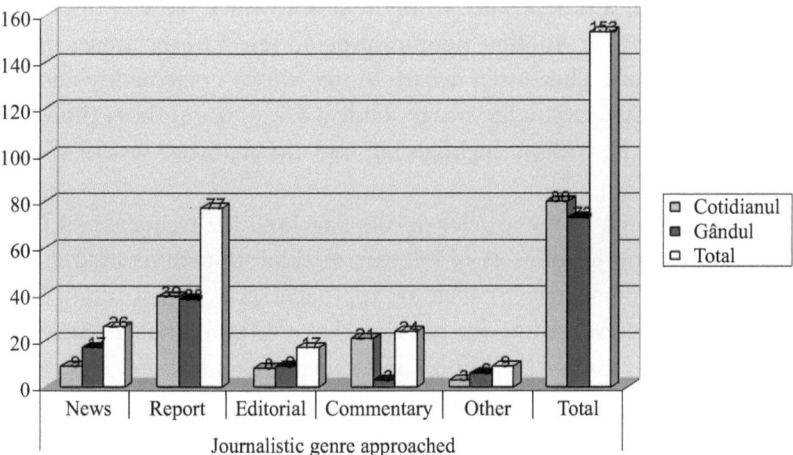

Frequency of journalistic genres approached

Thus, the news and reports counted for 103 of the 153 texts. *Gândul* is the newspaper that published the most such materials – 55 out of 73 – while in *Cotidianul* we found 48 articles out of 73. In the opinion articles chapter, 41 in total, the research showed that the *Gândul* publication keeps a more sober line, focused on the information and the event itself (only 9 editorials and 3 comments dedicated to revealing the Securitate files, the case of Mona Muscă), unlike *Cotidianul* which allocates a few pages daily to opinion articles. There we counted no less than 21 comments and 8 editorials that dealt with the subject in question. The fact should not be overlooked, however, that all editorials in the newspaper *Gândul* are published on the front page, in a privileged position and signed by Cristian Tudor Popescu, manager and opinion leader. Also, *Gândul* often publishes raw news from the *Mediafax* news *agency*. These materials respect some specific characteristics such as the strict structure of the inverted pyramid, the objectivity, and the rather small size.

At first glance, from the data obtained, we can conclude that the share of information-oriented articles is quite high, over half of the total. However, it should be emphasized that *Cotidianul* published several opinion pieces with a greater stylistic unity than that of news and reports which constitute, in a generalist daily, the basis of journalistic discourse. Also, the comments in this newspaper are often accompanied by relevant caricatures that give weight and relevance to the text and which we will discuss in the next subchapter. Another significant detail refers to the angles of the opinion materials. They often debate Mona Muscă's personality and the negative consequences on her image. Only a few of the authors choose to focus on the facts, without highlighting how the character was or should be affected.

The positioning of the articles on the page and the frequency of these placements were the subjects of another method of analysis used in this research. The importance of such an approach springs, first of all, from journalistic practice because the position that a certain article occupies on the page is relevant for the importance that the publication gives to the respective subject. This is because the first place the reader is tempted to look is *the optical center* of the first page – just above the middle of the page – in complete opposition to the place near the left edge of the publication, called the *spine* (Table 3, Appendix 1).

The research revealed that 66 of the 153 articles on the unfolding of events in the case of Mona Muscă were placed in the optical center, while only 13 were found near the *spine*. The remaining 74 articles were published on other pages of the two newspapers. With 41 articles centrally located, *Cotidianul* turned the case in question into a press campaign of the utmost importance, most of the impressions being consecutive and occupying significant space. The editorial team of the *Gândul* newspaper placed a total of 30 articles on the front page, of which 25 in the optical center and five near the edge.

It can be said that the newspaper *Cotidianul* gave greater importance to the subject, not only from the point of view of discussions but also from the point of view of the unfolding of events. Consistency in the transmission of the message on the first page determines the readers to include the information in the daily agenda of discussions, but it also exposes them, permanently, to the approach chosen by the journalists. Given the fact that the number of articles analyzed in the newspaper *Gândul* is 73 (compared to 80 in *Cotidianul*), we can reach the same conclusions in the case of this publication. An interesting detail is the fact that some of the articles placed in the optical center of the daily *Gândul* are editorials, whose attitude was mainly of condemning and accusing Mona Muscă in that context.

The frequency of the sections in which the articles appear (Table 3, *Appendix 1)* formed an analysis closely related to the page positioning of the articles because it is also part of editorial policy and journalistic practice in general. Thus, when an article is included in the page dedicated to *Current Affairs, it* means that the event is important enough to be found among the individual's priorities and can influence, in one way or another, their life. Due to these aspects, the reader will pay more attention to these materials.

Out of the sample of 153 articles subject to analysis, 52 texts occupied the *Current Affairs / Events* sector. The numbers of materials published by each daily are close: 29 in *Cotidianul* and 23 in *Gândul*. In the *Politics* section, 60 articles appear (38 – Gândul, 22 – Cotidianul), while 41 materials occupied the columns or pages reserved for *Opinion* (29 in *Cotidianul,* 12 in *Gândul)*. It is important that in the same newspaper issue the subject was not treated exclusively in a single section. Often, the frontpage event is commented both in the editorial and in commentary materials.

Following the observation of these data, we concluded that both publications conveyed to readers the message that the character of Mona Muscă, discussions about her Securitate files, as well as the events that followed, can influence their daily lives and must be carefully analyzed. The large share of articles in the opinion section, however, reveals that publications, especially *Cotidianul,* prefer to give great importance to the interpretation of reality and to deliver ready-made opinions and not information to the public. *Gândul* reserves less space for opinion, using mainly editorials for this purpose.

One of the most relevant analyses was the one through which we established the frequency of the article sizes (Table 5, Appendix 1). In general, journalistic space of any kind is limited, and the journalist is always in a position to choose which topic deserves the most typographic lines or minutes of broadcasting. Consequently, the chosen event must meet a series of criteria such as mainly temporal, but also spatial proximity, the prominence of the characters, or the implications of the case. Such an event cannot be overlooked by the constantly competing media institutions nor by those who receive the message – the target audience.

The events that formed the media campaign around Mona Muscă, as well as the comments on this information, were captured in journalistic materials with a length between 500 and over 6000 characters. However, the large materials, between 4500 and 6000 characters were predominant: 74. The editorial team of the *Gândul* newspaper preferred the long articles: 43 of the 74, and the journalists from *Cotidianul* published medium-length materials, between 3000 and 4500 characters (26 of the total of 35). *Gândul* is also the one that proposes most short articles, up to 1500 characters – 17 out of 27. We notice here that the editorial format adopted by this daily involves the publication of an editorial on a half column length, i.e., shorter than usual. Also, *Gândul* takes over news transmitted by the *Mediafax* news *agency*, these materials being smaller in size.

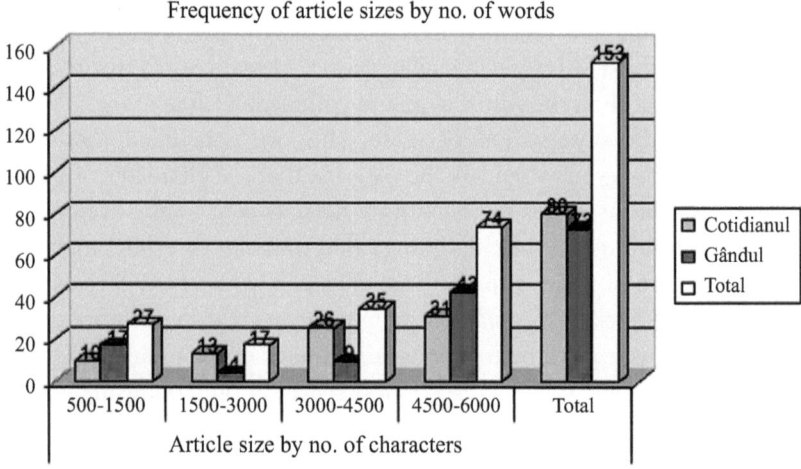

At this point we considered it necessary to make a comparative analysis between the number of opinion pieces, 41 in total, of which 29 in *Cotidianul,* and the predominant size of the articles (4500–6000 and more characters): 74 articles of which 31 in the newspaper mentioned. *Cotidianul* published editorials and especially commentaries on a printing area of comparable size or even larger than the area intended for information. The comments on those pages are signed by well-known journalists whose opinions are often considered landmarks by the target audience.

Since the research based on the analysis of the frequency of different elements such as the topics covered, the sections in which the articles appear or the positioning on the page was not enough to draw the expected conclusions, we performed an attitude analysis as shown in the sampled texts (Table 6, Appendix 1).

The approach involved dividing *the journalistic discourse* into three categories: *accusatory, neutral, and supportive*. The first and last groups were divided into three other subcategories, depending on the degree of discourse intensity: in *full, in part, and some places*.

Subsequently, we analyzed the 153 articles according to the keywords used, the message sent, and the tone of the texts. In conclusion, 83 materials were included in the category of Accusatory Discourse (34 – *Cotidianul*, 23 – *Gândul*), and 29 in Supporting Discourse (9 *Cotidianul*, 2 – *Gândul*). The remaining 41 fell into the Neutral/Balanced category. Subgroup fully accusatory *speech* counted 57 articles, compared to the fully *supportive speech* where we noted only 11 articles.

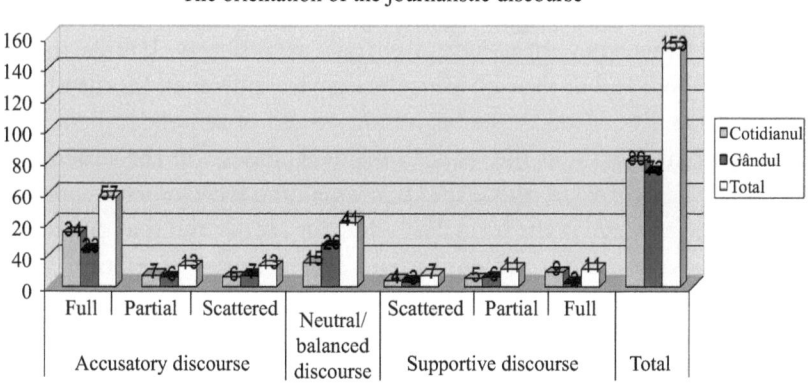

We easily noticed the predilection of the two dailies for a moralizing journalistic message, which would draw the public's attention to the character's mistakes and the consequences she must accept. Even when the public did not seem to assimilate the whole message, as evidenced by opinion polls, the newspapers maintained the same discourse, tending to marginalize that segment of the audience that did not seem to comply with what was published by the publications.

Gândul favored providing information through the materials dedicated to it, but it demonstrated a hostile attitude towards Mona Muscă through several consecutive editorials.

Journalistic deontology argues that opinion must be strictly delimited from information materials. However, some words, such as declarative verbs (*to claim* instead of *to say* or *tried to explain* instead of *explained*), the exclusive use of the family name or the replacement of the first name with the conspiratorial name (in this case: *Dana*), highlighted, on several occasions, the orientation of the publications and sent the reader a message which is difficult to notice at the conscious level, but which manifests its influence at the subliminal level.

These last observations opened the discussion on the analysis of the keywords that we carried out to enrich and clarify the present study. Besides, the issues we will present below have played an important role throughout the research, underlying the choices and conclusions.

The so-called *keywords* are the terms whose comprehension impacts the understanding of the whole sentence or even of the whole paragraph. Because of this, they must have a correct meaning, be known to the general public, and at the same time be easy to remember. Words of this type are usually placed at the beginning or end of sentences, being the elements that remain in the reader's memory and act at the subliminal level. The keywords are those that determine the receiver to decode the journalistic message in the form desired by the sender and that determine them to have a certain perception and a certain representation. This is due to the semantic sphere of the words that place the reader in the contexts desired by the authors. The abundance of keywords decreases the objectivity of journalistic discourse, a fact that is not very obvious on a conscious level.

On the contrary, *exact words* leave no room for interpretation and their dissection generally brings nothing new to the message conveyed.

Due to the influence that words can exert on the journalistic message, we analyzed the key terms observed in the sampled texts.

In the first stage of the work, we chose a series of words with impact in the context of uncovering the Securitate files and which were relevant in the case of Mona Muscă. The chosen terms and phrases guided the angle of approach and directed the journalistic message. Declarative verbs (*said, claimed, underlined,* etc.), nouns (*victim, snitch, guilt,* etc.), adjectives (*sincere, guilty,* etc.), or verbs (*acknowledged/did not acknowledge* or *tried*) determined the reception of articles in certain codes transmitted repeatedly to the reader. In the second stage, we followed the frequency of these words in the analyzed texts (Table 7, Appendix 1). To ensure the accuracy of the resulting data we used a program specialized in detailed language exploration, Concordance. With this, we checked, first of all, the word count, and, secondly, we followed the frequency of several words that formed the topics approached by members of the press.

Consequently, a total of 50,210 words resulted in the 80 articles taken from *Cotidianul,* out of which 9384 unique words and a total of 32860 words in the 73 materials from the *Gândul* newspaper, with 6923 unique words.

The phrase *secret police* and the acronym *CNSAS* were the most used expressions in the 153 articles, with 212 and 278 appearances, respectively. They were joined by phrases such as *conspiratorial name (code),* used 45 times, and *informative notes* – 30. All of these outline the context in which the events took place and raise, at the same time, a certain expectation for the reader. On August 12, *Cotidianul* published in the lead of an article: "*The informative notes* that Mona Muscă gave to the Securitate can only be made public by the victims," and the following sentence appears in the first lines: "Mona Muscă's main argument in the attempt to prove that she did not *engage in secret policing* was that she provided only verbal information." The repetition of the phrases determines an association of the character's image with the respective type of collaboration with the Securitate, all the more so since, until that moment, the National College for the Study of the Securitate Archives had not given any other *secret police collaboration* verdict.

The public is constantly kept in touch with the specific vocabulary of the Securitate. This is, first of all, the approach chosen by the editorial team of the *Cotidianul,* where the phrases *conspiratorial name* and *informative notes* appeared twice more often than in *Gândul*: 30 and 20 times. Due to this practice, the character constantly appears in a hostile context, whose recollection negatively influences the readers.

The word *file* is also very common in both publications, with the attributes: *the network* (54) and *surveillance* (40). "Regarding the collaboration of Mona Muscă, it can be assumed that the file refers to the activity that the MP had before 1989 at the Institute of Linguistics in Timișoara," *Gândul* published on August 9, before receiving the confirmation of the accusations submitted by Lavinia Șandru. This time, the newspaper seems to try to clarify the situation of the character and insists on the use of these phrases (40 and 34 times). *The network file* places the character among those who made a pact with the Securitate, and the character is often confused with this image. The public receives information that then comes under the influence of the mentality and personal prejudices about the communist regime and the secret services of those times.

To these are added the increased frequency of the word *snitch*, with the variant *ratted on*, which appeared a total of 45 times – 28 times in *Cotidianul* and 17 times in *Gândul*. This time, we are dealing with a harsh, penetrating word, which leaves no trace of interpretation, and which acts instantly both on a conscious level and on a subliminal level. The term has a direct impact on the words in its immediate vicinity and seems to annihilate any other phrase that could mitigate its effect. A good example is a statement with which an article from *Cotidianul* begins, dated August 11, 2006: "The most spectacular case is that of Mona Muscă, accused by a newspaper, after consulting three converging sources, that she was a Securitate *snitch* under the code name *Eva*," but also the title of a material published by the same newspaper on August 20, having as starting point the initial refusal of Mona Muscă to recognize the collaboration with the Securitate: "Why Do Snitches Keep Silent until They Are Found Out." Often, the word replaces the character's name, replacing it in the reader's memory.

Another relevant analysis is that of the verb *to admit* used in the perfect compound tense, affirmative and negative form. Thus, in the sampled texts, the verb was used nine times as *admitted* and 14 times as *did not admit*. The text conveys the message that the character preferred to deny the truth since the connotation of the verb implies the idea that the facts had already been proven at the time of the statement that comes to deny the obvious. For *admitted*, too, we are not dealing with a verb without connotations, once the impression given is that the sender came to make this confession after a struggle with her own conscience or because she is embarrassed by what she is about to declare.

Words such as *victim, sincerity,* or *transparency,* which would present Mona Muscă's image positively are less commonly used, compared to *mistake* or *guilt*. In the same sense, *morality* is replaced by its *lack*, and the adjective *moral* determines nouns used in contexts that show the reader how certain situations *should have been* but they are not in this case.

Mona Muscă's conspiratorial name, *Dana*, is used 49 times in the studied texts, *Gândul* being the newspaper that used the word 42 times. *Dana* replaces the character's name and surname in both titles and texts. "Lawyer Stoica Defends Dana for Free," *Gândul* headlines on September 21, 2006, or "The College Sent a Letter to SIE to Check Once Again if It Still Has Informative Materials from Dana" (end of the article from September 18).

If other expressions place the character in certain contexts, by using the code name in these ways, full identification with the character is achieved, who loses her previous image and acquires a new identity.

Declarative verbs are words that guide the tone of any journalistic material, even a news story or report, genres that normally do not allow the author's opinion to be revealed. *Saying* or *declaring* are neutral verbs that inform that the quoted sentences have been uttered. In contrast, verbs such as *try, claim,* or *emphasize* imply the opinion of the journalist who describes, subjectively, the statement made by his interlocutor. In the articles that make up the sample under analysis, the word 'said' was found 41 times (17 in *Cotidianul* and 24 in *Gândul*), while 'tried to' appears 13 times, 'claimed' five times, and 'pointed out' four times. On the one hand, the frequency of the verb 'said' indicates the objective presentation of statements, on the other hand, 'tried to' conveys the inability of the character to send a credible message and convince the audience. In addition, the audience notices the character's effort to express a certain thing that she fears or considers that she does not have the necessary power to convince the public.

We finalized the analysis of the keywords by observing the frequency of the terms *yes* and *no*, which set the tone of the journalistic discourse, determining the public to create a positive or negative perception, respectively, on the issue discussed in the text. *Yes* appeared 108 times in total, while *no* was counted 2023 times.

Following the content analysis, we can conclude that the sampled articles did not permanently retain an objective character. Neither the *Gândul* newspaper nor *Cotidianul* presented to the public only the course of events but tried to shape perceptions and build representations. The share of articles whose discourse accuses the character of Mona Muscă is much higher than the supportive ones, but also than the share of objective materials, which highlight the facts.

Cotidianul is the publication that tried to convey more opinions than news, most of the comments being based on a speech condemning the character and her attitude. Another important element is the fact that the newspaper *Cotidianul* was the one that published the open letter of Gabriel Liiceanu, addressed to Mona Muscă, a document written in a harsh language that was debated in several shows and publications. By becoming such a bridge of communication, *Cotidianul* did not encourage the pluralism of ideas and opinions, as it might seem at first sight, but promoted that kind of magnet materials for any type of audience. In this way, the series of articles took the form of a press campaign, the image of Mona Muscă being strongly affected.

The newspaper *Gândul* apparently kept a more sober line, characterized by the presentation of the events in detail. The typographic space given to this case was enviable compared to many other events, but we can note the predilection for the *Politics* section, where most of the articles were published, the first page is reserved for other current information. What led to the conclusion that *Gândul* did not have a balanced and objective journalistic discourse, were the texts of the editorials, which have the role of expressing the position of the entire publication. The editorials always had an accusing, moralistic tone that changed the perception of all the information transmitted.

In conclusion, we can say that through the published articles, the two dailies transmitted information to the public, but especially opinions and elements meant to manipulate public opinion by changing its perception.

In order to support what has been said, we will continue to analyze the titles of the articles and the images that accompanied most of the materials.

V.6. Analysis of the Headlines That Accompany the Studied Articles

For a more accurate analysis, we focused on the headlines published by the newspapers *Gândul* and *Cotidianul* between August 9, 2006, and September 20, 2006, an interval that we called *the key moment* of the events in the case of Mona Muscă. Thus, a sample of 73 titles resulted (46 in *Cotidianul* and 27 in *Gândul*).

A first observation was that the *Cotidianul* publication preferred the verbal titles ("Lavinia Talked: You Too, Mona!?" from August 9 or "PNL Snitches Join Another Network" – August 19), while *Gândul* published predominantly titles from which the verb is missing: "Mona Muscă: Better with Securitate than Communist" – Aug. 17; "Too Late and Too Early," editorial from August 23.

On the one hand, the verbal titles maintain the connection of the reader with reality and individualize the act of communication. The verb ensures speech dynamics and draws attention to the utterance. On the other hand, some titles from which the verb is missing create the feeling of expectation, incite, and invite the reader to read at the same time.

With few exceptions, *Gândul* chose to publish informative headlines, which announce and summarize the news or report: "CNSAS Verdict: Mona Muscă Was a Secret Police Collaborator" – September 19. The same event was titled by *Cotidianul* as follows: "Verdict: Secret Policewoman." We notice how publications juggle with the noun *verdict*. In the first case, the word is well determined and does not mislead the public in any way, while in the second case, the term leaves room for interpretations from which the wrong conclusions can be drawn; the headline does not specify the person or institution that gave the verdict.

By the previous example, we highlighted the fact that the *Cotidianul* newspaper preferred incentive headlines, which attract the reader and sometimes promise to offer them more than the information contained in the article, which contradicts journalistic deontology: "Errata: Eva is Dana" – August 11, "Snitching for Dummies" – August 17, "Queue at Confession" – August 23.

Regarding the proper names used in the titles, we can retain even from the previous examples the tendency to replace the character's name with the conspiratorial name and the creation of puns on this topic. *Mona* becomes *Dana* or even *Eva*, even though the existence of the code name *Eva* had not been certified on that date. Memorable is the title published by *Gândul* on August 11: "Mona Muscă Admitted: She Is "Dana," A Colleague from the Securitate." The word *colleague* suggests a close relationship, if not friendship.

Also, many of the titles place Mona Muscă in non-existent contexts unrelated to the events, and whose connotations have an impact on her public image, which is clearly damaged – "Mona Muscă, Swept Out by PNL," published in *Gândul* on August 15 or "Traian Băsescu and the Mona-Dana Typhoon" that appeared in *Cotidianul* on August 14. We notice here that with the unfolding of events, both in texts and in titles, a phrase like *Mrs. Mona Muscă* was replaced by the name *Muscă*, often using the expressions used by Gabriel Liiceanu in his open letter: "The Talented Mrs. Muscă and the Ecstasy of Lying." The expressions were found as such, but they also served as a source of inspiration for several leads and texts published during that period.

Among the terms used mostly in the headlines of the two dailies are the keywords discussed in the content analysis. Among those, the lexical families of the verb *to rat out* and the noun *Securitate* are most often exploited with various meanings: "Snitching for Dummies" – August 17, "Mona Poured Sorrow and Amazement into the Soul of The Elite" – August 16, "The Securitate Between Beatings and Literary Comments" – September 18 – *Cotidianul*; and "PNL Gets Rid of Snitches" – August 29, "Trips to CNSAS Restore Mona Muscă's Securitate Memory" – August 23, from *Gândul*. However, there are other expressions whose significance affects the verticality of the character: "Mona Confuses the Dissidents," August 23, *Cotidianul*. The headline brings a serious accusation, the size of which is not substantiated in the article.

Most of the titles accuse the character, insinuate her guilt and the consequences that Mona Muscă should assume. The sentence-like headlines are also highlighted, the content of which is not, in line with the information contained in the article every time ("The Dirtbag You Are Trying to Call Is Out of Coverage Area," *Cotidianul*, Aug 26).

In conclusion, the titles chosen by the two editorial teams highlight, much more clearly than some of the articles, the opinions of the authors and the direction in which the journalistic discourse is heading. The low frequency of purely informative or narrative headlines illustrates the daily newspaper's attempt to attract as large an audience as possible at the expense of the image of the character being written about, namely Mona Muscă. This analysis reveals the intention to manipulate shown by the two dailies, a trend manifested, we believe, especially for financial purposes. The permanent competition between the publications determines a sensationalist approach of the events, the consequences on the players being immediately felt.

V.7. Analysis of the Images Placed Next to the Researched Articles

The statement *a picture is more telling than 1000 words* has become almost a cliché due to repeated use in recent years. However, this does not prevent print journalists from attracting their audience, first of all, through visual elements and, only afterward through content. A generalist newspaper, which does not favor gossip, must face the competition by publishing photos closely related to the event, but which leave an impression due to their originality. In most cases, press photography is a redundant element, which helps to visualize the facts presented and which remains in the reader's memory.

Some publications choose to introduce other types of images, such as cartoons, which, since they enter the sphere of opinion, give the author the freedom to express himself. Theoretically, this should be done without harming the public image of the caricatured ones. As we will see below, some cases deviate from this deontological norm.

To perform this analysis, we selected four significant images from each of the two dailies. The editorial policy of the newspaper *Gândul* presupposes that the published images are, for the most part, black and white photographs that capture the character mentioned in the next article. The publication does not give much importance to the image, the text being the privileged one and the element that occupies most of the page. However, the photos used are chosen in such a way that they convey both an obvious and a subliminal message.

Cotidianul has a different approach in this regard. Here too, the photos are not used in excess, instead, the opinion articles are accompanied by colorful caricatures, as suggestive as possible. The images sometimes cover half a page, being a real point of attraction for the reader.

Given these observations, we decided to analyze a group of relevant photographs from the newspaper *Gândul* (August 9, 10, 11, 2006) and a symmetrical group of caricatures that appeared in the pages of *Cotidianul* (August 14 and 16, September 4, 2006). Most of the selected images are part of the same *key moment* of the events in the case of Mona Muscă, like the titles under analysis. However, we also considered it useful to add the images published on the day when Mona Muscă received the final verdict of CNSAS and announced her retirement from political life (March 7, 2007).

The first of the photos from *Gândul* accompanies the article with the title: *Mona Muscă, Caught In "Network Files,"* published on the day when MP Lavinia Şandru declared to the press that Mona Muscă collaborated with the Securitate.

The photo is probably an archive one and is an exception to the editorial rule of the daily *Gândul*, being in color. At the first level of reception, we notice that the character is caught in profile, with her index finger up, a favorite position for most of the photos that were published during that period. In the background, the Romanian flag appears. The connotation of this photo starts from the symbolism of the flag – an element of national identity, whose importance increased after leaving communism and which alludes to the devotion displayed by Mona Muscă towards some aspects

Analysis of the Images Placed Next to the Researched Articles   105

of Romanian life. The raised finger, however, denotes demagoguery, the attempt to impose a certain point of view. On closer inspection, the finger actually seems to support the deputy's head. In this case, the position corroborated with the grimace displayed creates the impression that the character is deep in thoughts and at the same time disgusted by what is seen/heard. It is worth mentioning the option for a photo whose main character looks to the outside of the article, which is considered an error in journalistic practice.

The photo next to the August 10 article, entitled "Mona Muscă Defended Herself Against the Accusations of Collaboration, Claiming that She Lives in an Apartment Building," capturing the character from the bottom up, an angle which is unflattering most of the time, but which normally emphasizes the importance of the one photographed or filmed (photo 1, *Appendix 2)*. The foreground is occupied by the profile of a palm that could belong to Mona Muscă, having the role, as in the previous example, to strengthen the deputy's speech. But the palm may also belong to a reporter who is waiting to ask a question. Note the serene expression of the character correlated with the statement quoted in the first lines of the article: "we have not collaborated with the secret police for a second," a statement made trivial by the fact that it was placed under the ironic headline of the article.

One of the most interesting images, which conveys an obvious message both denotatively and connotatively, is the one that appeared on August 11, under the title of high impact "Mona Muscă Acknowledged: She Is "Dana," a Colleague of the Securitate."

This time, too, the character is caught in profile, probably while upholding her point of view before the CNSAS members. The reader can locate the scene due to the acronym placed on the sheet placed (through a technical artifice) next to Mona Muscă. We notice the position of the lips that seem to articulate the word "no," a perception that immediately connects, in the collective subconscious, with the sentence present at that time in all press and television materials: "we have not collaborated with the secret police for a second." Another detail is the accentuated contrast between the white outfit of the character and the black in the background, a contrast present in the other photos as well. White – the color of purity, which conveys the impression of sincerity – is in opposition to the fatal, telluric black.

To illustrate Mona Muscă's decision to withdraw from the Parliament and the Liberal Democratic Party, the newspaper *Gândul* chose a dynamic photo, possibly from an archive, which makes the entire article redundant (photo 2, Appendix 2). Mona Muscă is depicted walking towards the exit of one of the halls of the Parliament, leaving behind a deserted council table. From a connotative point of view, the photograph reveals that the character has lost much of her support and has to bear the consequences of her actions.

The images chosen by *Cotidianul* are much more plastic, based on a not very subtle irony, with a pronounced sententious character. The cartoons that precede the comments from August 14 and 16, respectively ("Romanian Negationism, How We Became a Peacemaker") are graphically similar and are built around the protagonist Mona Muscă. We also notice here the appearance of Adrian Năstase, in both drawings, along with the message according to which, the PSD politician would have some advantages following the forced withdrawal of Mona Muscă due to the circumstances.

The first caricature (photo 3, Appendix 2) exploits the antithesis between good and evil, angel and demon while transmitting a subtle message. Thus, the protagonist transformed into the Devil descends to the flames of her own files, raising, at the same time, the *angels* Năstase, Stănoiu, Voiculescu, and Vadim Tudor – characters whose collaborations with the Securitate are notorious. The author emphasizes their dubious innocence through the gesture of Adrian Năstase, who throws accusations at Mona Muscă, lowering her to Hell. Impartially, the postman angel Dinescu approaches this seesaw that defies the laws of gravity, holding a symbolic envelope, from the College, on which is written triumphantly: CNSAS Sunday.

The caricature effect is the same as that of the illustrated seesaw. A paradoxical one. Even if it is obvious that the situation should evolve in favor of Mona Muscă, the existence of the files and the interests of the *angels* that led to their appearance determine her fate. The symbol of the Devil, underlined by the 666-shaped tail and the horns of the character, is much stronger than the political games suggested by the drawing. The reader who does not have the time or knowledge necessary to analyze the caricature in detail or to read the text carefully receives and keeps, subconsciously, the obvious message based on popular logic: *you were in the wrong, now you are paying.*

The second selected drawing (photo 4, Appendix 1) is one of the few that illustrates Mona Muscă as a victim of the communist regime. The reason for the crucifixion appears here, the cross being symbolically represented by a sickle and a hammer. The same elements serve as weapons in the hands of those in charge of the last moments of Mona Muscă's political career: Gabriel Liiceanu and Adrian Năstase (we discussed above the message referring to the latter). The protagonist is caught in white clothing – an allusion to her statements – which, in conjunction with religious references, places the character in a positive light. However, her expression does not have much in common with that of the Savior, Mona Muscă being irritated by Adrian Năstase. The Divine Aura is blurred, and the scene of the crucifixion is trivialized.

This caricature was published on September 4 under the title "Great Romanian Liars" and conveys one of the clearest messages in *Cotidianul*.

Mona Muscă is portrayed as Pinocchio, the little boy brought to life by his creator and well known for his lies. Even if Pinocchio is not a Romanian character, the phrase *your nose will grow like Pinocchio's* is often used, recalling the story according to which the nose gave him away as a liar. The whole image complemented by the book held by Mona Muscă – *Innocent and Patriotic Reports* – mocks her conviction that the notes given to the Securitate were well-intentioned and emphasizes the character's attitude of permanent denial.

If the *Gândul* newspaper presented Mona Muscă on the day of her retirement from political life, leaving a deserted room, *Cotidianul* does not offer her an alternative: both on the left and the right, the road is closed with *the secret police* signs (photo 5, Appendix 2). The protagonist heads resolutely towards one of the ends. The expression on her face is harsh, sharp, and denotes determination and anger at the same time. The message sent to the reader does not imply any regret and highlights Mona Muscă's refusal to accept the CNSAS decision.

The analysis of these images leads to the conclusion that the publications kept the message from the articles at a visual level as well. Both *Gândul* and *Cotidianul* propose photographs that have a secondary purpose to informing the public: that of creating new perceptions and representations, consequently manipulating the public opinion in the direction desired by the two dailies. *Gândul* maintains the line of less involved discourse that we have noticed in the analyzed texts. The photos are innuendoes but do not affect the image of the character. *Cotidianul*, however, practices more incisive journalism, as confirmed by the expressive caricatures, which build a negative perception of the case and personality of Mona Muscă.

CHAPTER VI: Conclusions

We opened this paper with the definitions of *information* – the unit that underlies any journalistic approach. Raw information does not represent the exclusive prerogative of the members of the press, each individual being constantly surrounded by certain data that they have to understand and model according to their own needs. However, the media are such institutions whose purpose is to take over and process information that is relevant and useful for a wide, heterogeneous, and versatile public. we said at the beginning of the paper that information itself is an abstract notion, in the absence of context. That is why the media take up the information that underlies certain events. We are therefore dealing with contextualized information.

The journalist is the one who chooses, processes, and issues a message corresponding to each fact classified as an event, which meets the necessary criteria to become news and to enter, in the end, the attention of the public opinion. The audience represents the final target of the information transformed into journalistic material. And the purpose of the media is twofold: both to inform and to make a profit – with the exception, in theory, of national television. Any means of communication, public or private, should play the role of public service which includes the dissemination of data, public education, and entertainment. Sometimes, however, financial reasons take precedence, making profit a priority, especially in the case of commercial media. This is just one of the reasons why certain slippages occur in the way reality is reflected in press materials.

As discussed above, *disinformation* is one of the ways in which the press can mislead the public. This is sometimes done to serve certain interests of the journalist, owner, or political interests, while other times disinformation occurs following involuntary mistakes, omissions caused by poor documentation, or lack of professionalism. The consequences depend on the affected audience segment, but also on the subsequent behavior of the radio/television station or publication, which may deny or simply come back with corrections on the wrongly or superficially treated subject.

A more serious and dangerous form of misleading the public is *manipulation*. This is a premeditated act of causing one or more persons to act in the direction desired by an individual or group. The first tier of manipulation is manifest at the level of perception undergoing changes, later felt in opinions, and finally in decisions and actions. As the main message bearers in contemporary society, the media can convey information and especially opinions that favor certain points of view and ignore those that are contrary to them. This happens when the media serve, as in the case of disinformation, interests other than those of the general public. Manipulation is performed by various methods, of which granting a longer broadcasting time or typographic space and discrediting through negative press campaigns are the most common.

This way of manipulating public opinion often finds its place in media scandals that have long-term or even indefinite consequences for those involved.

This paper analyzed how the written press treated a subject that gave rise to multiple media campaigns: the presentation of the events that formed the case of Mona Muscă, at the time of declassification of her Securitate files.

In this sense, we submitted to the analysis a sample consisting of 153 articles taken from the newspapers *Gândul* and *Cotidianul*. The choice of publications was made according to the type of target audience and because the editorial teams include well-known trainers and opinion leaders. Following the content analysis performed and the observations made on the qualitative data, we were able to reach several relevant conclusions.

The research highlighted the editorial policy approached by the two dailies starting from the predominant type of journalistic discourse. *Gândul* mostly maintained its objectivity, both at the level of text and at the level of images. The message sent is focused on the event and the information behind it. Headlines are those editorial elements that best convey the opinions of journalists. The case of Mona Muscă was followed daily, and the articles occupied large areas of the page. Despite the objectivity found in the information materials – except for the headlining – the repeated editorials, placed in the optical center of the first page, surprised a hard, accusing, and often defamatory position towards Mona Muscă. Given these observations, we concluded that the newspaper tried to manipulate the target audience by attacking Mona Muscă's person, which led to the deterioration of her public image.

In the case of *Cotidianul,* the research results were clearer. This was due to the editorial policy of the newspaper which allows a more subjective approach to both opinion and information materials. The public was constantly exposed to articles accusing Mona Muscă and condemning her deeds. The intention to manipulate the public was especially manifested in images and especially the caricatures that accompany the comments in *Cotidianul.* Visual data are more easily received both consciously and subliminally, the message they convey often changing the audience's perceptions. Throughout the press campaign, Mona Muscă was caricatured in various poses, depending on the turn of events. The drawings suggested scenarios and gave verdicts, often to the detriment of the character.

The analyzed press segment revealed the predilection for a speech condemning Mona Muscă. The message received by the target audience was not a balanced, objective one, but one that contradicts the deontology of the journalistic profession. The audience was influenced by repeating the same idea in several consecutive articles, followed by images meant to affect the image of the character. People who accessed the forums of the analyzed newspapers showed negative reactions to Mona Muscă during and after the media scandal, and the results of the polls conducted following the press campaigns revealed a 30 percent decrease in the population's trust in Mona Muscă. Given these arguments, we believe that the publications tried to manipulate public opinion, which affected the social image of the character.

The analyzed example represents a slippage of the written press, which could have been caused by a series of internal factors, related to the beliefs of the editorial teams, but also external – political interests. We emphasize that articles were also found that adopted a balanced speech or even in support of Mona Muscă, which leads to the conclusion that manipulation is not the rule of the journalistic profession.

APPENDIX 1

Table 1. Coding of the orientation arising from the analyzed articles

Variable	Code
1. Objective presentation of information	1
2. Condemnation / accusation of the character	2
3. Condemning the deeds of the Securitate (in general)	3
4. Support for the character	4
5. The character mentioned in passing, without influencing the article	5
6. Launching of hypotheses	6
7. Others	7

Table 2. Frequency of journalistic genres

Name of the daily	Journalistic genre					Total
	News	Report	Editorial	Comment	Other	
Cotidianul	9	39	8	21	3	80
Gândul	17	38	9	3	6	73
Total	26	77	17	24	9	153

Table 3. Frequency of page positioning of articles

Name of the daily	Page positioning			Total
	Home (in the optical center)	Home (next to "spine")	Another page	
Cotidianul	41	8	31	80
Gândul	25	5	43	73
Total	66	13	74	153

Table 4. Frequency of the sections in which the articles appear

Name of the daily	Section			Total
	Events / Current affairs	Political	Opinion	
Cotidianul	29	22	29	80
Gândul	2. 3	38	12	73
Total	52	60	41	153

Table 5. Frequency of topics in the selected articles

Variable	Cotidianul		Gândul		Total
	Number	Percentage	Number	Percentage	
1. Objective presentation of information	15	18.75	26	35.61	41 (26.7 %)
2. Condemnation / accusation of the character	34	42.5	2. 3	31.5	57 (37.2 %)
3. Condemning the deeds of the Securitate (in general)	4	5	3	4.1	7 (4.5 %)
4. Support for the character	9	11.25	2	2.73	11 (7.1 %)
5. The character mentioned in passing, without influencing the article	12	15	12	16.43	24 (15.6 %)
6. Launching of hypotheses	2	2.5	2	2.73	4 (2.6 %)
7. Others	4	5	5	6.84	9 (5.8 %)
Total	80	100	73	100	153

Calculation of the attitude index according to the formula: TA = (F − U)/L, where:
TA = trend analysis index
F = number of favorable units
U = number of unfavorable units
T = total number of units
TA Cotidianul = (9−34)/80 = − 0.3125
TA Gândul = (2−23)/73 = − 0,2876
TA Total = (11−57) / 153 = − 0.3

Table 6. Orientation of the journalistic discourse

	Accusatory			Neutral / balanced speech	Supportive speech			Total
	Full	Partial	Scattered		Scattered	Partial	Full	
Cotidianul	34	7	6	15	4	5	9	80
Gândul	2. 3	6	7	26	3	6	2	73
Total	57	13	13	41	7	11	11	153
	83				29			

APPENDIX 1

Table 7. Frequency of item sizes depending on the number of characters

Name of the daily	Item size depending on the number of characters				Total
	500–1500	1500–3000	3000–4500	4500–6000 ≥	
Cotidianul	10	13	26	31	80
Gândul	17	4	9	43	73
Total	27	17	35	74	153

Table 8. Distribution of keywords within the selected articles

Word / Phrase	The name of the daily		Total
	Cotidianul	Gândul	
1. snitch; (to) rat out	28	17	45
2. secret police	112	100	212
3 conspiratorial / code names	30	15	45
4. informative notes	20	10	30
5. CNSAS	80	198	278
6. collaborator; (to) collaborate	87	53	140
7. network file (s) to be tracked	14/6	40/34	54/40
8. victim	12	4	16
9. morality / morals	16	18	34
10. guilt	15	9	24
11. mistake	4	3	7
12. sincerity / honesty	8	5	13
13. transparency	7	2	9
14. admitted / did not admit	6/10	3/4	9/14
15. Dana	7	42	49
16. Eva	8	2	10
17. said	17	24	41
18. pointed out	2	2	4
19. claimed	5	-	5
20. tried	10	3	13
21. yes	84	24	108
22. no	1578	445	2023

APPENDIX 2

Transposition into graphics (elements that were not included in the publication): tables above.

1.

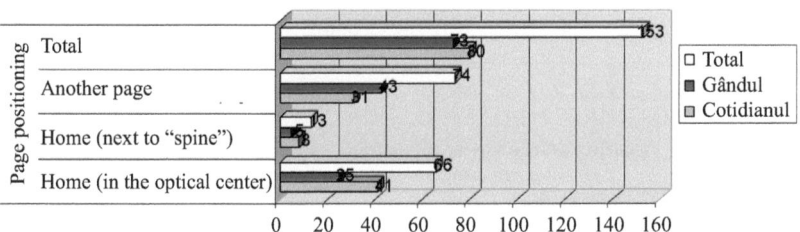

Frequency of page positioning of articles

2.

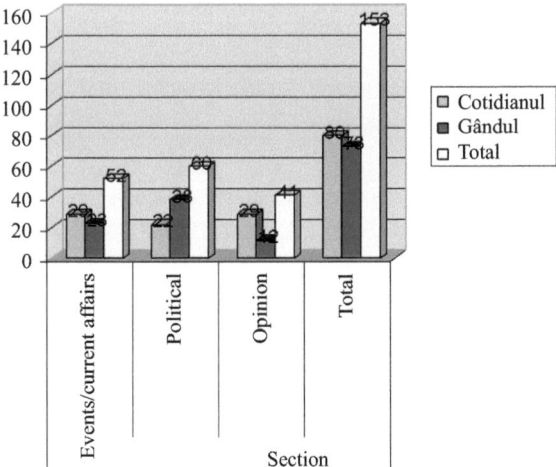

Frequency of the sections in which the articles appear

APPENDIX 2

3.

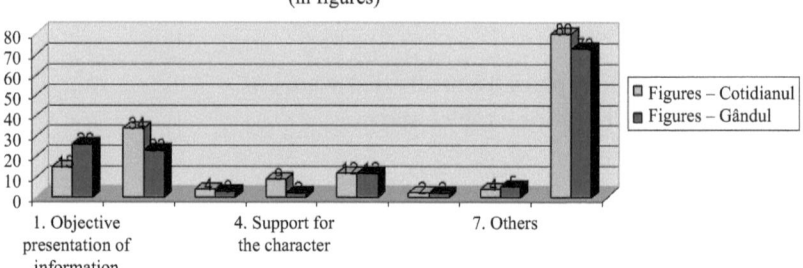

4.

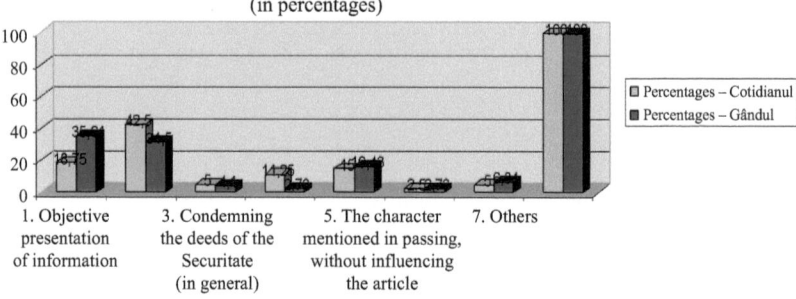

5.

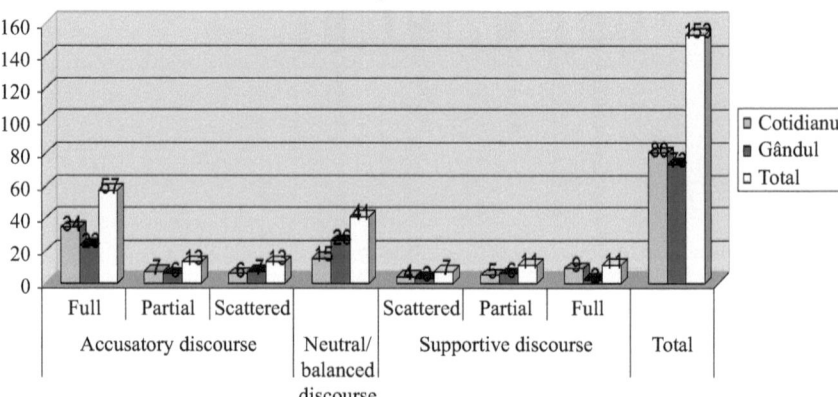

APPENDIX 2

6.

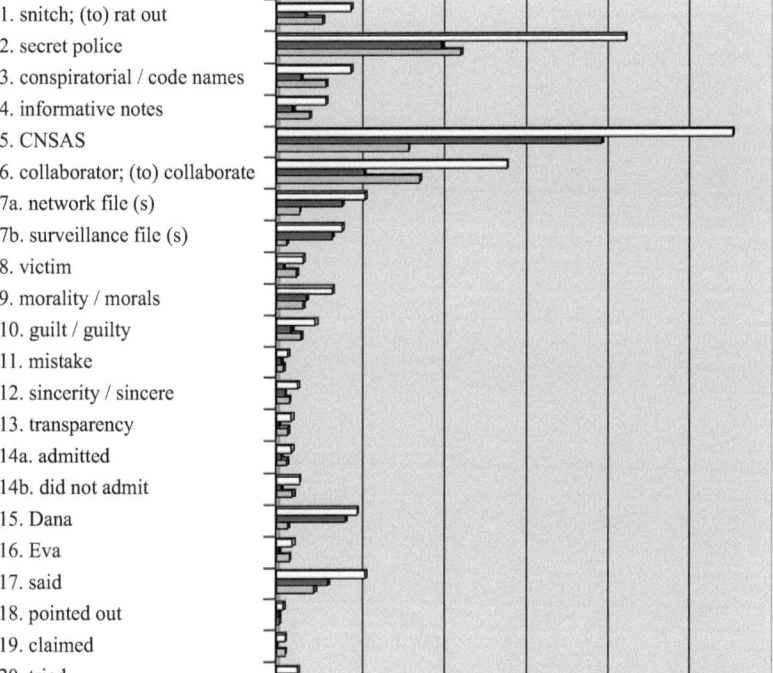

Distribution of keywords within the selected articles

1. snitch; (to) rat out
2. secret police
3. conspiratorial / code names
4. informative notes
5. CNSAS
6. collaborator; (to) collaborate
7a. network file (s)
7b. surveillance file (s)
8. victim
9. morality / morals
10. guilt / guilty
11. mistake
12. sincerity / sincere
13. transparency
14a. admitted
14b. did not admit
15. Dana
16. Eva
17. said
18. pointed out
19. claimed
20. tried

- Cotidianul
- Gândul
- Total

APPENDIX 3

Photo 1

Photo 2

Photo 3

124   APPENDIX 3

Photo 4

Photo 5

APPENDIX 4

Mona Muscă's political career:

- in 1990, she became a member of the "Civic Alliance," and between 1991 and 1995 she was a member of the National Council of the CAP and headed the Department of Image and Public Relations
- in 1995, she joined PNL, where she headed the Image and Media Department
- in 1996, she was elected deputy for Caraş-Severin, on the CDR lists
- between 1996–2000 she was vice-president of PNL
- from May 2000, alternate member of the Delegation of the Romanian Parliament to the OSCE Parliamentary Assembly
- 2001–2005: member of the Executive Bureau of the PNL
- December 2004, Minister of Culture in the Tariceanu Government
- July 2005: resigns from the position of minister and vice-president of PNL, in protest against the Prime Minister's decision not to resign, in order to organize early elections
- between December 2004 and January 2005, she is a member of the Permanent Bureau and vice-president of the Chamber of Deputies
- initiator of the draft laws on free access to Information, of the legislative proposal on the organization and operation of the Rompres National Press Agency, of the draft law on lustration or of the one on the conflict of interests in exercising public functions and dignities
- member of the Commission for Culture, Art, Mass Media
- Member of the Committee on Equal Opportunities for Women and Men (since February 2006).
- on August 8, 2006, Lavinia Şandru, deputy of the National Initiative Party, publicly declared that the Mona Muscă file had reached CNSAS.
- On August 14, 2006, the PNL Central Permanent Bureau decided to withdraw political support for Mona Muscă. Mona Muscă was subsequently expelled from the PNL (on 2 September 2006 and lost her observer seat in the European Parliament)

- on November 29, 2006, joins the Liberal Platform led by Theodor Stolojan, transformed into the Liberal Democratic Party in December 2006
- On March 7, 2007, Mona Muscă announced that she was resigning from the Parliament and the Liberal Democratic Party, following the CNSAS decision that she collaborated with the secret police, recently sanctioned by the Court of Appeals.

Bibliography

1. Agabrian, Mircea, *Content Analysis*, 2006, Bucharest, Polirom.
2. Bertrand, Claude-Jean ed.,*An Introduction to the Written and Audiovisual Press*, 2001, Iași, Polirom.
3. Chelcea, Septimiu, *Public Opinion: Persuasion and Manipulation Strategies*, 2006, Bucharest, Economica.
4. Chiciudean, Ion and Țoneș, Valeriu, *Image Crisis Management*, 2002, Bucharest, Comunicare.ro.
5. Coman, Mihai ed., *Introduction to the Media System*, 1999, Bucharest, Polirom.
6. Coman, Mihai ed., *Journalism Manual* Vol. I, 2001, Iași, Polirom.
7. Coman, Mihai ed., *Journalism Manual* Vol. II, 2001, Iași, Polirom.
8. *Larousse Media Dictionary*, 2005, Bucharest, Encyclopedic Publishing House.
9. DeFleur, Melvin L. and Ball-Rokeach, Sandra, *Theories of Mass Communication*, 1999, Iași, Polirom.
10. Dobrescu, Paul and Bârgăoanu, Alina, *Mass Media and Society*, 2003, Bucharest, Comunicare.ro.
11. Ficeac, Bogdan, *Manipulation Techniques*, 2004, Bucharest, Politica.
12. Joule, R.V. and Beauvois, J.L., *Manipulation Treaty*, 1997, Bucharest, Antet
13. Nasty, Vlădoiu, *Information Protection*, 2005, Bucharest, Triton.
14. Popescu, Cristian Florin, *Explanatory Dictionary of Journalism, Public Relations and Advertising*, 2002, Bucharest, Triton Publishing House.
15. Popescu, Cristian Florin, *Journalism Manual*, 2005, Bucharest, Tritonic.
16. Randall, David, *Universal Journalist*, 1998, Iași, Polirom.
17. Rémy, Rieffel, "Mass-media and Political Life" in Bertrand, Claude-Jean ed., *An Introduction to the Written and Audiovisual Press*, 2001, Iași, Polirom.
18. Săftoiu, Claudiu, *Political Journalism*, 2003, Bucharest, Three.

19. Stan, Sonia Cristina, *Manipulation Through the Press*, 2004, Bucharest, Humanitas.
20. Volkoff, Vladimir, *Short History of Disinformation*, 1999, Bucharest, Antet.
21. www.cotidianul.ro
22. www.gandul.ro

Index of Names

A
Agabrian, Mircea 84–86
Asch, Solomon E. 50

B
Ball-Rokeach, Sandra 27, 28, 33, 56, 57
Balle, Francis 56
Baylon, C. 24
Bârgăoanu, Alina 26, 27, 38, 39, 77
Beauvois, J.L. 44, 45, 47, 48, 53
Bernays, Edward L. 55
Bertrand, Claude-Jean 9, 19, 31–34, 36–38
Besson, Patrick 29
Berelson, Bernard 16, 59, 86
Blumler, J. 27
Bogart, Leo 28
Burke, Edmund 7

C
Cantril, Hadley 26
Cathala, Henri-Pierre 21
Cazeneuve, Jean 37, 55
Cialdini, Robert B. 48–53
Chelcea, Septimiu 23, 24, 41–44, 47–53, 55, 59, 85
Chiciudean, Ion 74–77
Clausse, Roger 13
Coman, Mihai 13–17, 19, 26–29, 32–38, 56–60

D
DeFleur, Melvin L. 27, 28, 33
Dobrescu, Paul 26, 27, 38, 39, 77

Drăgan, Ion 27, 55, 56, 58
Durand, J. 35

E
Ellul, Jacques 23, 38

F
Ficeac, Bogdan 41, 45–47, 53, 54
Fiske, John 56, 57
Fraser, Scott C. 48
Freedman, Jonathan L. 48
Freund, Andres 14

G
Gerbner, Georg 60
Gouldner, Alvin 51

H
Hertzog, H. 27

J
Jakobson, Roman 18
Joule, R.V. 44, 45, 47, 48, 53

K
Katz, Elihu 27, 59
Kientz, Albert 18

L
Lasswell, Harold D. 9, 32, 84
Lazarsfeld, Paul 16, 26, 27, 36, 59
Lee, A.M. 52
Lee, E.B. 52
Legris, Jacques 29, 30
Lenain, Pierre 41, 42
Lewin, Kurt 14

Levinson, Hary 77
Lippmann, Walter 38, 39
Lull, J. 57

M
Machlup, Fritz 10
McLuhan, Marshall 35, 37
Maffessoli, G. 37
Mancher, Melvin 14
Mathien, M. 32
McQuail, Dennis 13, 19, 28, 56
Merlino, Jacques 31
Merton, R.K. 16, 32, 36, 50
Miege, Bernard 54
Mignot, X. 24
Moles, Abraham 18
Muchielli, Roger 75

N
Nasty, Vlădoiu 11
Noelle-Neumann, Elisabeth 58

P
Pavlov, Ivan P. 52
Piaget, Jean 47
Popescu, Cristian Florin 13, 14, 18, 21, 23, 55, 82, 83, 91
Porat, Marc U. 10
Postman, N. 38

R
Randall, David 14
Rădoi, Mireille 11–13
Reardon, K.K. 42
Rémy, Rieffel 28

S
O'Sullivan, Tim 56, 60
Săftoiu, Claudiu 7, 69–73
Severin, W.J. 56, 60
Simons, H.W. 50
Shannon, Claude E. 9, 12
Stan, Sonia Cristina 55, 61–63

T
Tankard Jr., J.W. 56, 60

V
Volkoff, Vladimir 21–27, 29–31

W
Weaver, Warren 9
Weimann, Gabriel 59
Wells, H.G. 26
Wiley, Malcolm 13
Woodrum, E. 84
Wright, C.R. 17

Z
Zimbardo, Philip 46

Studies in Politics, Security and Society

Edited by Stanisław Sulowski

Vol.	1	Robert Wiszniowski (ed.): Challenges to Representative Democracy. A European Perspective. 2015.
Vol.	2	Jarosław Szymanek: Theory of Political Representation. 2015.
Vol.	3	Alojzy Z. Nowak (ed.): Global Financial Turbulence in the Euro Area. Polish Perspective. 2015.
Vol.	4	Jolanta Itrich-Drabarek: The Civil Service in Poland. Theory and Experience. 2015.
Vol.	5	Agnieszka Rothert: Power of Imagination. Education, Innovations and Democracy. 2016.
Vol.	6	Zbysław Dobrowolski: Combating Corruption and Other Organizational Pathologies. 2017.
Vol.	7	Vito Breda: The Objectivity of Judicial Decisions. A Comparative Analysis of Nine Jurisdictions. 2017.
Vol.	8	Anna Sroka: Accountability and democracy in Poland and Spain. 2017.
Vol.	9	Anna Sroka / Fanny Castro-Rial Garrone / Rubén Darío Torres Kumbrián (eds.): Radicalism and Terrorism in the 21st Century. Implications for Security. 2017.
Vol.	10	Filip Pierzchalski: Political Leadership in Morphogenetic Perspective. 2017.
Vol.	11	Alina Petra Marinescu: The Discursive Dimension of Employee Engagement and Disengagement. Accounts of keeping and leaving jobs in present-day Bucharest organizations. 2017.
Vol.	12	Jacek Giedrojć: Competition, Coordination, Social Order. Responsible Business, Civil Society, and Government in an Open Society. 2017.
Vol.	13	Filip Ilkowski: Capitalist Imperialism in Contemporary Theoretical Frameworks. 2017.
Vol.	14	Leszek Leszczyński / Adam Szot (eds.): Discretionary Power of Public Administration. Its Scope and Control. 2017.
Vol.	15	Tadeusz Klementewicz: Understanding Politics. Theory, Procedures, Narratives. 2017.
Vol.	16	Tomasz Bichta: Political Systems of the Former Yugoslavia. 2018
Vol.	17	Miroslav Palárik / Alena Mikulášová / Martin Hetényi / Róbert Arpáš: The City and Region Against the Backdrop of Totalitarianism. 2018
Vol.	18	Jolanta Itrich-Drabarek / Stanisław Mazur / Justyna Wiśniewska-Grzelak (eds.): Understanding Politics. Theory, Procedures, Narratives. 2017.
Vol.	19	Jerzy Juchnowski / R. Jan Sielezin / Ewa Maj: The Image of "White" and "Red" Russia in the Polish Political Thought of the 19th and 20th Century. Analogies and Parallels. 2017.
Vol.	20	Roman Kuźniar: Europe in the International Order. 2018.
Vol.	21	Piotr Jaroszyński: Europe - the Clash of Civilisations. 2018.
Vol.	22	Stanisław Filipowicz: Truth and the Will to Illusion. 2018.
Vol.	23	Andrzej Szeptycki: Contemporary Relations between Poland and Ukraine. The "Strategic Partnership" and the Limits Thereof. 2019.

Vol. 24 Sylwester Gardocki / Rafał Ożarowski / Rafał Ulatowski (eds.): The Islamic World in International Relations. 2019.

Vol. 25 Jacek Zaleśny (ed.): Constitutional Courts in Post-Soviet States. Between the Model of a State of Law and Its Local Application. 2019.

Vol. 26 Andrzej Antoszewski / Przemysław Żukiewicz / Mateusz Zieliński / Katarzyna. Domagała: Formation of Government Coalition in Westminster Democracies. Towards a Network Approach. 2020.

Vol. 27 Joanna Osiejewicz: Global Governance of Oil and Gas Resources in the International Legal Perspective. 2020.

Vol. 28 Anita Oberda-Monkiewicz: Poland-Mexico towards a Strategic Partnership. 2020.

Vol. 29 Bartosz Czepil / Wojciech Opioła: Ethnic diversity and local governance quality. The case of Opole Province in Poland. 2020.

Vol. 30 Adam Szymański / Jakub Wódka / Wojciech Ufel / Amanda Dziubińska: Between Fair and Rigged. Elections as a Key Determinant of the 'Borderline Political Regime' - Turkey in Comparative Perspective. 2020.

Vol. 31 Tomasz Grzegorz Grosse (ed.): Fuel for Dominance. On the Economic Bases of Geopolitical Supremacy. 2020.

Vol. 32 Dariusz Jarosz / Maria Pasztor: From Subjection to Independence. Post-World War II Polish-Italian Relations. 2020.

Vol. 33 Paweł Sekuła: Chernobyl Liquidators. The Unknown Story. With the Testimony of the President of Latvia. 2020.

Vol. 34 Kamil Glinka (ed.): Urban Policy System in Strategic Perspective: From V4 to Ukraine. 2020.

Vol. 35 Paweł Lesiński: At the Origins of German Liberalism: the State in the Thought of Robert von Mohl. 2020.

Vol. 36 Jana Popovicsová (ed): Reflexions about a Cultural and Social Phenomenon: Identity. 2020.

Vol. 37 Agnes Bernek: Geopolitics of Central and Eastern Europe in the 21st Century. From the Buffer Zone to the Gateway Zone. 2021.

Vol. 38 Marek Antoni Musioł: The European Union as a Post-Lisbon Regional Security Complex. 2021.

Vol. 39 Alina Petra Marinescu: Manipulation in the Disclosure of the *Securitate* Files. The Case of Mona Muscă. 2021.

www.peterlang.com

www.ingramcontent.com/pod-product-compliance
Ingram Content Group UK Ltd.
Pitfield, Milton Keynes, MK11 3LW, UK
UKHW041922210426
5322IPUK00002B/5